A Little Drama!

A Little Drama!

Playful Activities for Young Children

Lavinia Roberts

Redleaf Press®
www.redleafpress.org
800-423-8309

Published by Redleaf Press
10 Yorkton Court
St. Paul, MN 55117
www.redleafpress.org

First edition 2018
Cover design by Erin Kirk New
Cover photographs by ozenli/iStock
Interior design by Louise OFarrell
Typeset in Chaparral Pro
Interior photos by Tom Martin
Printed in the United States of America
25 24 23 22 21 20 19 18   1 2 3 4 5 6 7 8

Library of Congress Cataloging-in-Publication Data
Names: Roberts, Lavinia, author.
Title: A little drama! : playful activities for young children / Lavinia Roberts.
Description: First edition. | St. Paul, MN : Redleaf Press, 2018 | Includes
    bibliographical references.
Identifiers: LCCN 2017056136 (print) | LCCN 2018016166 (ebook) | ISBN
    9781605545868 (ebook) | ISBN 9781605545851 (pbk. : alk. paper)
Subjects: LCSH: Drama—Study and teaching (Early childhood)
Classification: LCC PN1701 (ebook) | LCC PN1701 .R57 2018 (print) | DDC
    372.66/044—dc23
LC record available at https://lccn.loc.gov/2017056136

Printed on acid-free paper

To

Jennifer Van Bruggen Hamilton and the Topeka Civic Theatre

William Inge Center for the Arts

Wendy Barrie and the community of Trinity Wall Street Parish

ArtsConnection & ProjectArt

Behind every great teacher are great teachers. Special thanks to
Dr. David Montgomery, Tony Graham, Dr. Nancy Smithner,
Regina Ross, Ralph Lee, Dr. Amy Cordileone, Dr. Daphnie Sirce,
Javier Cardona, James Miles, and Alexander Santiago-Jirau

My loving parents, Mary and Richard Roberts, who nurtured
my love of the arts and helped me become the educator
and artist I am today

Contents

Preface xi

Part One: Introduction to Drama in Early Childhood and Directing Young Actors to Success 1

. . . .

Chapter One: Introduction and Teaching Pedagogically 3

Why Is Drama So Important in Early Childhood? 3

Curtain Up! Ways to Incorporate Drama in the Classroom 5

The Instructor's Role in Drama Class 7

Creating Community 8

Introducing Drama to Your Classroom 9

Classroom Tips 12

The Importance of Structure in Drama Class 13

Chapter Two: Tools to Get Everyone Centered and On Track 17

Positive Classroom Management Strategies or Centering Activities 17

Part Two: Building a Drama Class 21

. . . .

Chapter Three: Breathing Exercises and Techniques 23

Various Breaths 23

Breathing Exercises 27

Chapter Four: Vocal Warm-ups 31

Vocal Warm-up Activities 32

Chapter Five: Warm-ups for the Mind and Body 39

Concentration, Focus, and Listening Warm-up Activities 39

Energizing Warm-up Activities 50

Chapter Six: Imaginative Play 61

Imaginative Play Activities 62

Chapter Seven: Creative Movement 79

Jump and Jive! Creative Movement Activities 82

Chapter Eight: Cooldowns, Reflection Tools, and Closing Rituals 101

Cooldown Activities 101

Reflection Activities 106

Curtain Call! End-of-Class Rituals 108

**Part Three: Incorporating Music, Art, and Literature
into the Drama Classroom 111**

· ·

Chapter Nine: Incorporating Music 113

Incorporating Musical Instruments 114

Activities Using Musical Instruments 115

Create Musical Dramas Using Popular Children's Songs 120

Drama Activities Based on Popular Children's Songs 120

Incorporating Classical Music 123

Activities Inspired by Classical Music 123

Chapter Ten: Incorporating Visual Art 135

Incorporating Visual Art Projects into Drama Class 136

Drama Inspired by Famous Paintings 138

Dramatic Activities Inspired by Visual Artwork 140

Chapter Eleven: Incorporating Literature: The Storybook Drama 149

Bringing Together Drama and Literacy 149

Dramatizing a Storybook in Class 149

Using a Storybook in Drama Class 157

Part Four: Bringing It All Together 173

Chapter Twelve: Devising Plays with Pre-K 175

What Is Devising? 175

The Rewards of Devising 177

Crafting a Creative Collaboration 178

Themes for Creative Collaborations 178

On Your Mark . . . Get Set . . . Setting! 179

Creating a Character 179

Once Upon a Time . . . Story Time! 181

Improvise 183

Pen to Paper 183

The Role of the Narrator 184

Face the Audience and Project That Voice! 185

X Marks the Spot! 185

Stage Business 186

Practice Makes Less Scary 187

A Little Song and Dance! 187

Set Crew! 188

Costume Creation 188

Rolling Camera! 188

It's the Journey, Not the Destination 188

Curtain Call! 189

Reflection 189

Curtain Up! 189

Example of a Twelve-Class Devising Schedule 190

Queenie's Birthday: A Play by a Pre-K Drama Class 191

Appendix 195

Sample Lesson Plans 196

Blank Lesson Plan Template 212

Glossary of Terms 217

Bibliography 219

Preface

I first taught early childhood education at Topeka Civic Theatre and Academy in Topeka, Kansas, one of the largest community theatres in the country. We created storybook dramas based on folktales from around the world, such as Jabutí, the tortoise from the Amazon basin, or mongoose, a trickster from folklore of the Maasai, the indigenous people of Kenya. My teaching practice was dedicated to cultivating the troupe's voices, bodies, and hearts, as well as allowing the class to explore and play in the world of the folktale. I deeply appreciated how exuberant and willing to be creative these young actors were, and this experience began my love of working in early childhood education.

My passion for creating theatre with young people brought me to New York City to pursue graduate studies in Theatre Education for Colleges and Communities from New York University. I have continued to develop my teaching practice, teaching both visual art and theatre in child care centers, churches, professional theatres, art centers, and public and private schools. I have worked with such arts organizations as Wingspan Arts, ProjectArt, the Children's Art Guild, Writers Theatre of New Jersey, Urban Arts Partnership, ArtsConnection, and others. I have taught toddlers to adults, but I continue to love creating work with very young children.

While teaching in early childhood spaces, I noticed the lack of drama programs in New York City in both public and private schools. Many had a drama center as part of their classroom centers, which allowed child-initiated dramatic play. Yet few used drama to teach curriculum or had community-created and community-centered drama activities as an active part of their curriculum.

As an educator who was teaching drama to young children, I was also startled by the lack of activity books and resources for teaching drama to young children. Many contained wonderful pedagogy but lacked activities and practical advice for implementing dramatic activities in an early childhood space.

I knew that I wanted to write a book for busy educators, especially those without a theatre background, about how to incorporate drama in their early childhood classrooms. I wanted a book where a teacher could easily find a drama activity or create an entire drama lesson to teach whatever topic the children were learning about in school. A book where teachers could easily find what they were looking for.

I have a multidisciplinary approach to teaching theatre, one that incorporates elements of visual art, yoga, music, and dance. People learn in different ways, and there is immense value to exploring a topic using various art forms. Yoga can be a wonderful way to focus the class and warm up the body for drama play or cool down the body at the end of a drama class. Music can help set the mood or environment of a dramatic activity. Creating sets, puppets, and costume pieces for drama class during art class will bring the drama even more to life for young children. Creative movement ignites the imagination and helps the body create a new vocabulary of expressive movements while developing gross-motor skills.

I hope that my curriculum and teaching pedagogy will nurture, empower, and ignite your imagination and those of the young people you teach.

PART ONE

Introduction to Drama
in Early Childhood and
Directing Young Actors
to Success

CHAPTER ONE

....

Introduction and
Teaching Pedagogically

Why Is Drama So Important in Early Childhood?

Including dramatic play in an early childhood classroom is extremely nurturing to the social, emotional, and physical development of young children. Drama is an exciting way to teach children and can be incorporated into other subjects such as reading, science, music, and visual art. Drama classes are also a wonderful way to develop a nurturing and supportive community in your classroom. Including drama in your curriculum also promotes self-expression and develops empathy. Drama is a wonderful tool to nurture the minds, bodies, and hearts of young children.

Social Development

Whether playing a drama game as an entire class or in small groups during centers, theatre promotes prosocial behaviors in young children. Prosocial behaviors can be divided into three main categories: sharing, helping, and cooperation. Displaying sympathy and kindness, positive verbal and physical contact, and empathy are also important prosocial behaviors (Preusse, accessed 2017).

When young children do dramatic play in centers, they must work together to decide roles, find props, and create the setting and story for the drama together. When doing drama as a larger community, children must all participate and support the others in the group for the drama to be successful. This type of cooperative, theatrical play helps children learn how to communicate verbally with others to express their ideas and needs. The young children must also reach compromises with their peers so the drama class is mutually beneficial for all participants. By nurturing prosocial behaviors, early childhood educators are helping young children develop the tools that will help them interact with adults and their peers in a beneficial and appropriate manner (Preusse, n.d.).

Drama play, in large or small groups, can also be an opportunity for children to reflect on the world around them and draw from their own experiences and observations. According to Bredekamp and Copple in *Developmentally Appropriate Practice in Early Childhood Programs*, "Children do not construct their own understanding of a concept in isolation but in the course of interaction with others" (1997, 114). Young children will create dramatic play experiences set at school, at home, on public transportation, at a museum, at a zoo, and even at a restaurant. By giving children the opportunity to explore the world around them with their peers, you are providing the children with a safe space to reflect on and process their own life experiences in a fun and creative environment.

Incorporating drama into the early childhood classroom nurtures critical-thinking skills. Children will have to problem solve as a community as they participate in some drama activities, such as deciding who will be what character during a drama center game of dress-up. While pantomiming how to make a peanut butter sandwich or turning the drama center into a restaurant, children will reflect on the world around them. During the end-of-class reflection, they can critically deconstruct that day's events, problems they encountered, and the solutions they devised. Reflections also provide them with the space to reflect on how they would do activities differently, or alternative solutions they didn't use but could employ moving forward. Reflections can also be a space where children share and discuss questions that arose from that day's drama class. Classroom activities—both play-based and structured—that encourage children to reflect, predict, question, and hypothesize will teach them to be creative, critical, and independent thinkers.

Emotional Development

A drama classroom is a safe and judgment-free space for children to explore and express difficult emotions like anger, sadness, fear, and jealousy. Theatre can help children become more emotionally intelligent and comfortable and aware of their own emotions, which will help them later in life when dealing with difficult emotions and in understanding others who are dealing with difficult emotions; empathy helps individuals connect with others and understand their feelings and behavior (Allison et al. 2011). Drama cultivates empathy in young children as they pretend to be others and reflect on the feelings and experiences of others during drama class and dramatic play. According to Parvin Parsai's dissertation, "A Case Study of Preschool Children Exhibiting Prosocial and Empathic Behaviors during Sociodramatic Play," pretend play promotes empathy in young children:

> When children engage in pretend (or dramatic) play, they are experimenting with the social and emotional roles of life, an important element in emotional development, also known as emotional competence. That is, children learning to be in tune to their own emotions, understand, and express their own feelings to others; all precursors to developing empathy—the understanding the emotions of others, and relating to others with greater sensitivity. (2014, 23–24)

Parsai goes on to discuss how research demonstrates that children who participate in dramatic play have more empathy toward others because these children directly experience being someone else for a short period of time (24). They also gain the skills to better cooperate with peers, control their impulses, and be less aggressive than young children who do not engage in dramatic play (Dodge, Colker, and Heroman 2002).

Physical Development

Individuals with high kinesthetic intelligence process information through their bodies, using muscle, sensation, and movement to explore and learn. For young children who learn primarily kinesthetically, their bodies are their avenue to learning and understanding any content or subject. Movement is also their preferred form of self-expression (Gardner 2006). Drama can be a key educational tool for kinesthetic learners. Drama games often involve creating gestures or movements along with dialogue and words. Creative movement activities and body warm-ups are very popular with kinesthetic learners.

Drama also promotes young children's physical development: Many physical warm-ups promote fine- and gross-motor skills and eye-hand coordination. Concentration games, such as relaxing breathing techniques, give children helpful tools to focus, self-regulate, and calm their bodies. Creative movement activities promote children's bodily awareness and expressing their feelings through their bodies. Drama also promotes fitness in a way that is noncompetitive and fun for individuals with a wide range of abilities and aptitudes; it teaches children to be aware of and attuned to their own bodies. Movement helps young children develop spatial skills and nonverbal communication skills (Poole, Miller, and Church). During a creative movement game, for example, children become more aware of others' bodies in the space, which helps them develop spatial awareness and personal boundaries.

Curtain Up! Ways to Incorporate Drama in the Classroom

There are a variety of ways that you can incorporate dramatic play and drama into the lives of young children. Try to incorporate a blend of teacher-led and student-led drama activities, as well as allowing students to engage in drama class with an entire class and to engage in dramatic play alone and in independent groups. Although many activities in this book are centered on larger group activities—both student-and teacher-led—aim to cultivate these different types of drama experiences in your classroom. These different environments and types of drama play will nurture young children in different ways that are important to their development.

Solitary Dramatic Play

Allow children to play alone, creating different characters using costume pieces and playing with the props. It's important for children of all ages to have self-directed play and time by themselves. During this time, they can intensely focus, reflect, and imagine (Anderson-McNamee and Bailey 2010). Often, when children are ready they will reach out to others to join in.

Dramatic Play in Small Groups

Give children the space to create skits and plays together to promote interpersonal intelligence and language skills. Children must discuss what characters will be in their dramatic play and negotiate who will play what. Children must listen to each other and work together to play in a way that is fulfilling and meets the needs of everyone involved. Children will have to communicate their thoughts and needs to the group.

If children have difficulties working together, you can facilitate this play by offering suggestions, helping them reach compromises, and playing with them as a peer by being a teacher-in-role, discussed below.

Community-Centered Drama Play

Community-centered activities are focused around teamwork, inclusion, and fun. During some of these activities, children are working together to complete a task or goal. For example, during "Count Down and Up" (page 41), a warm-up activity, children are working together to keep a ball in the air and count to ten as a class. During several drama activities in this book, such as, "1, 2, 3, Repeat after Me" (page 27) in chapter 3, or "Number Echo" (page 35) in chapter 4, children will take turns leading a drama activity by creating the sound or movement the rest of the class will follow. While one child is leading, the other children are developing their observational and listening skills; in this way, all children are participating and engaged all the time.

Teacher-in-Role Drama Play

A teacher-in-role means that you will play a character during a particular theatre activity. Perhaps you are Old MacDonald visiting the different animals, played by your class, on Old MacDonald's farm. Maybe you are Little Bo-Peep looking for her sheep—your students—who are hiding around the classroom. As teacher-in-role, you will facilitate and move the drama forward by pretending to be a character. You do not always need to be a teacher-in-role, but for certain activities it's a good idea to give yourself a character and to ask the class pertinent questions to guide the narrative forward collectively. Children enjoy having their teacher be part of the drama activity, and they will take the activity more seriously if they see that you too are invested and trying your best. You will make the imaginative world of the drama activity more real for children, which will nurture their imaginations.

Child-Centered Drama Play

Cultivate a classroom culture where children lead the drama class. Ask them questions to decide what will happen next in the drama. Pause to allow them to reflect on the drama. Ask them questions about the imaginative world of the drama. What sounds do they hear in the forest? What do the birds sound like? Let them make important decisions regarding who will play what character in a drama. Give them as much ownership of the space as you can while still maintaining a safe and structured space. Allowing children to create skits and performances gives them confidence and allows them to guide and take charge of their own learning. Allowing children to make choices is a vital part of early childhood education: When children are presented with choices, they can practice the skills of independence and responsibility, while their caregivers and educators can guard their health and safety by keeping surveillance of their choices (Maxim 1997). Young children's attention spans will likely be longer if they choose an activity themselves rather than being assigned a task by the teacher, without choices (Grossman, accessed 2017). Giving children choices promotes self-esteem, cognitive development, and a feeling of control and ownership.

Know your kids. What are their needs? What are their cultural backgrounds? What are their interests? What questions do they have that you could explore in drama class? How can you incorporate their needs and interests into your drama curriculum? The more that students' interests and needs are addressed, the more the children will be engaged and invested in drama class, bringing passion and enthusiasm to every lesson. Additionally, they will bring their own knowledge and experiences into the drama class, enriching the process for the entire class.

The Instructor's Role in Drama Class

Your role as a teacher in a drama environment is vital. You will bring the energy and set the stage for drama class. Here are some suggestions on how you can flourish and be the best possible teacher:

- Be a mediator to help children who are engaged in dramatic play as a group but who are experiencing conflict to reach an equitable solution that reflects and meets the needs of everyone in the group. Help them express their needs to the rest of the group and practice listening to their peers, as well as brainstorming possible solutions to disagreements.

- Always be child-centered.

- Always participate in every activity. Doing this models how to do the activity and creates a positive classroom community.

- An important rule of improvisation is to say yes. During dramatic activities, say yes as much as you can to children's suggestions for class.

- Move on to the next activity when children are emotionally ready to move on.

- Try to keep class sizes to less than fifteen children.

○ Embrace yourself and your teaching style. What strengths do you bring? Are you calm and nurturing? Are you zany and gregarious? What cultural background or interests do you have? What makes your style special? What music brings you joy? Share yourself in your teaching practice.

Creating Community

Creating a strong and safe community provides the wings for young children to really fly during drama class. When children feel safe and supported—emotionally, intellectually, and physically—by their teachers and their peers, they will invest fully in drama class. A larger sense of community will also drive young children to work together to achieve the task or goals of the drama game. Here are some suggestions for creating an affirming and nurturing community in your drama classroom:

○ There are many activities that involve being in a circle. Warm-ups and reflections are best done in a circle. This allows everyone to see each other, which promotes learning from and being inspired by observing peers, a sense of community, and equality.

○ Emphasize the process of drama play over the product.

○ Do theatre activities that promote students working together to achieve something and are not about elimination or competing to be the winner.

○ Activities that involve students taking turns encourage children to be respectful listeners and audience members, and they also give students an opportunity to speak in front of classmates and lead the drama class. Still, be careful when taking turns: students often prefer to do things together, as it's less scary than speaking alone and it keeps everyone engaged.

○ Create a brief class contract or continue to use the class contract that is already in place in your classroom. One talented actor and teaching artist has a class contract for drama classes that reads:

• be safe with our bodies

• be safe with our hearts

• participate

You can ask students if they can do each of these things, and even discuss them briefly. Ask the children if they can do each of these items individually, and then do a high five out into the middle of the circle for each one, similar to a sports team cheering each other on. Have only one or two rules that are easy to remember, such as "one mic, one voice," or "treat others as you want to be treated." Make discussing rules fun and engaging, such as having the students jump ten times if they can treat others how they want to be treated.

Introduce your children to drama by creating a drama center, if you don't already have one, and doing group-centered drama activities. Both are important and help nurture different developmental needs.

There are sample lesson plans in the appendix on page 196 that will help you create lesson plans for a forty- to forty-five-minute drama class. Do not feel you need to follow these lesson plans. Perhaps drama class is only ten minutes long, consisting of an opening and closing ritual, warm-up and cooldown, and one drama activity. Perhaps you will not create a formal drama class component in your classroom day, but you will add some cooldown activities before naptime (see chapter 8). Maybe some dramatic activities will become part of your morning circle ritual. Perhaps you will use some of the literacy activities during story time (see chapter 11). Use these activities as they meet the needs of your community and classroom. Whether your drama class is teacher-initiated or student-led drama, or runs ten minutes or forty minutes, make sure to establish a clear ritual and structure so young children know what to expect and anticipate for drama class.

Facilitating drama class can be emotionally, physically, and intellectually demanding. You are physically participating in all the activities while still watching the children for their safety, as well as using your emotional intelligence to pick up the emotional energy of the community. Have compassion for yourself and have fun as you create or enhance your drama center and/or start planning how to incorporate dramatic activities into your classroom curriculum!

Drama Center

A drama center is an important part of any early childhood classroom or child care center. Create a space that is dedicated to young children engaging in solitary and peer-led dramatic play. Provide them with various supplies to create engaging dramas with their peers or by themselves.

Recommended supplies for a drama center include various items such as the following:

o costume pieces

o props

o any set pieces, either created by the children, such as a mural of a garden, or a ready-made set piece, such as a toy oven

o a puppet theatre and puppets

Maintaining a Drama Center

o Rotate items in the center to reflect the themes being explored in the class, seasons, or the children's current interests.

○ Try to choose nongendered costume pieces, if possible.

○ Allow children to create set pieces using large cardboard boxes. Let the children create murals on large rolls of white paper or brown butcher paper based on what they are currently learning about.

○ Create puppets in visual art class that can later be used in the drama center. There are a variety of different kinds of puppets children can make at this age, including brown-bag puppets, finger puppets, shadow puppets, and sock puppets.

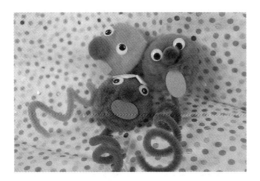

Drama center themes could include the following:

○ kitchen

○ restaurant

○ fairy tale

○ veterinarian's office

○ a day at the beach

○ grocery store

○ toy shop

○ doctor's office

○ post office

○ toy shop

○ flower shop or garden

○ a day at the farm

○ art museum or art gallery

○ outer space and astronauts

○ woodland creatures

○ a day at the zoo

○ on a safari

○ camping

○ hair salon

○ construction workers and builders

Recommended Supplies for Teaching Drama

Following is a list of supplies you can use to teach drama class. You can also make some of these supplies available in the drama center for children to play with on their own:

- sheer handkerchiefs for creative movement
- hats and other headgear for dramatic play and community theatre games centered on developing children's imaginations
- puppets and a puppet stage (can be homemade: a table turned on its side, a strung-up curtain, brown paper taped between two chairs, etc.)
- a prop box with various props, perhaps themed around what students are learning in school
- shakers
- Hula-Hoops
- beanbags
- music
- various costume pieces (These can be donated by families or picked up at a thrift store. Young children enjoy wearing vintage items. Even an old bandana can inspire a fun character. Be creative and open-minded when creating a classroom costume box.)
- an essential oil diffuser, to help children warm up or calm down their bodies. Diffusers are great for breathing exercises or during warm-ups and cooldown.

Calming Scents

bergamot	frankincense	peppermint	sandalwood
chamomile	lavender	rose	

Energizing Scents

cinnamon	grapefruit	orange	tangerine
eucalyptus	lemon	pine tree	tea tree
ginger	lemongrass	rosemary	thyme

There are many other essential oils you can use to assist in energizing or calming children. Try different blends and combinations of oils to create unique smells. Avoid using incense or candles; open flames shouldn't be in the classroom. Invest in organic, fair-trade essential oils for your diffuser. Some essential oil diffusers also change colors, and you can turn down the lights in the classroom to create a really meditative and calming atmosphere. Make sure that none of the children are sensitive to any scents before using.

Everyone brings unique experiences, gifts, and perspectives to their teaching practice. Here are some tips for teaching drama. Use whatever is helpful to you and your classroom.

- Place stickers or tape on the floor in a circle so students can find their spot when you say, "Let's make a circle." Here is a popular circle rhyme with early childhood educators: "C-I-R-C-L-E, do I see a circle in front of me?" Say the rhyme until everyone is in a circle. You can also say, "Circle time," and snap to the tune of *The Addams Family* theme as the chorus, with the verse being the following:

  > Standing straight and tall,
  > My feet don't move at all,
  > We're having such a ball,
  > Hooray! It's circle time!

- Young actors should never get "out" or be made to compete in theatre games. Drama activities should be centered on working together and building community, not competition!

- Thank actors for making good choices to build an affirmative and supportive space. Often, other actors will make better choices because they, too, want to receive affirmations. Affirmations are an excellent way to promote students making good choices.

- Consider having a reward system in place. When someone makes a good choice in drama class, explain why and reward them with the title "Superstar." A reward for being a superstar can be as simple as getting a star sticker at the end of class and having the student's name written on the board under the title "Drama's Superstars of the Day!" Try to find an opportunity for everyone to be a superstar, whether it's for listening, participation, or a positive attitude. This is a great way to acknowledge each child's special contribution to the space.

- Provide consistency and class rituals in drama class. Rituals are comforting and let young children anticipate what to do next in class. Having lessons that are structured the same way will create class routines.

- Don't be afraid to give students a couple of friendly reminders about the classroom's community contract if they are not making the best choices.

- If students are shy or uncomfortable with an activity, respect their feelings and allow them to observe or say, "No, thank you." Usually, when they see what fun the other participants are having, they will join in at a pace and in a way that reflects their needs and what is comfortable for them. Always validate and respect a young person's feelings. Often, shy students will go after everyone else if you ask them again at the end of the activity. It gives them time to warm up and see how fun the activity is.

- Teachers, if able, should always do every activity, no matter how strenuous and silly, whether it's rolling on the floor or making monkey noises. This models and mentors to the young actors how to do the various activities and keeps everyone engaged and connected.

- Don't be afraid to repeat a step as many times as necessary or stop an activity to help the group focus.

The Importance of Structure in Drama Class

It is always good to start with a focus activity to bring everyone in the drama class together. Next, warm up the body, voice, heart, and mind for drama class. Complete an imaginative play activity to spark the children's minds and a creative movement activity to nurture their bodies and hearts. Conclude with a cooldown and a final reflection. Children need to prepare their voices, hearts, minds, and bodies for drama, and they need to cool down their bodies and reflect on their experiences so they can move on with their day.

Each chapter in this book will go into detail about the types of activities you can do during the different parts of a drama class. Sample lesson plans themed around the four seasons are located in the appendix (page 196). Feel free to do a few extra focus activities or multiple creative movement activities if children need to move. Also, children may want to vary the activities they do depending on what time of day you have drama class. These are your students and you know their needs.

Routines and Rituals in the Drama Classroom

Providing consistent structure is an important part of any drama class's daily routine, which is different from a ritual. A routine is "a repeated, predictable event that provides a foundation for the daily tasks in a child's life" (Gillespie and Peterson 2012, 76). Routines help young children know intuitively what comes next, which helps with classroom management. Routines are vital to actors of all ages but especially young actors. Routines provide safety, comfort, and structure.

Rituals, although similar to routines, are defined as "special actions that help us navigate emotionally important events or transitions in our lives as well as enhance aspects of our daily routines to deepen our connections and relationships" (Gillespie and Peterson 2012, 76).

For example, a routine in a pre-K drama class is to always begin and end with a circle-time song. This ritual emotionally engages children in the drama class, connects the community, and signifies the beginning and end of drama class. Rituals deepen the connection between teachers, children, and their peers and nurture an engaged and supportive community. A ritual that emotionally connects the children might be everyone standing in a circle at the end of drama class and patting themselves on the back, giving the whole class a round of applause, or doing a group high five. Rituals show appreciation and respect for the others in the community and acknowledge the space and time the children are sharing together. Every moment educators and children have together is an opportunity to nurture a positive relationship (Ostrosky and Jung, 1). Create a drama class routine and meaningful, emotionally engaging rituals that strengthen the community in your classroom.

Elements of an Early Childhood Drama Lesson Plan

Each chapter will highlight different components of a well-structured drama class. See appendix (page 196) for sample lesson plans.

Theme/Learning Goals: What are children exploring and learning about today? What would you like the children to accomplish today? What skills would you like to cultivate or introduce? What would you like the children to take away from today's lesson? The theme could be inspired from what children are learning in other classes, such as music, art, science, or literacy. For example, if they are learning about metamorphosis in science, drama class can be themed around metamorphosis and the experience of being caterpillars and butterflies.

Materials: A list of materials you will need for that day's lesson. Might include visual images, music, props, musical instruments, or costume pieces. It's beneficial to have all supplies prepped before class and ready to hand out but out of sight, if possible, to help the activities move quickly. Consider having a drama bag that contains that day's supplies and taking materials out with a dramatic flourish to reveal what you will be using that day.

Opening Circle and Breathing Activity: Bring actors' minds and bodies to the present so actors can get ready to experience drama class. These activities also bring the children into a circle together to create a sense of community and togetherness. These activities can be found in chapter 3.

Vocal Warm-up: Loosen up the voice and prepare it for drama class. These activities can be found in chapter 4.

Concentration, Focus, and Listening Warm-up: Help actors focus on the present moment and develop active listening skills and mindfulness. These activities can be found in chapter 5.

Energizing Body Warm-up: Prepare the body for drama class. These activities can be found in chapter 5.

Imaginative Play Activity: A drama activity that engenders and nurtures imagination and creativity. These activities can be found in chapter 6.

Creative Movement Activity: An activity that allows students to move creatively with their bodies. These activities can be found in chapter 7.

Cooldown: Allows children to cool down their bodies and refocus their minds to the present. These activities can be found in chapter 8.

Closing Circle and Reflection: Allows children to process and discuss their experience and gives you the opportunity to get feedback about what the children got from the drama class. These activities can be found in chapter 8.

Closing Ritual: A ritual that signifies an end to drama class. These activities can be found in chapter 8.

Using This Book

Throughout this resource book, you will see terms used repeatedly during each activity:

Materials: Materials are any supplies that you may need to assemble for a given activity.

Act it out! Step-by-step instructions on how to facilitate an activity.

Encore! Ideas explaining how to extend the activity, either through variations or into art, music, or story time.

Director's notes: Helpful hints about how to facilitate each activity or where to use an activity in a drama lesson.

Spotlight on: Informs the reader which of the six early learning domains the activity nurtures:

- cognitive
- physical and motor development
- creativity and the arts
- approaches to learning
- language and literacy
- social and emotional learning

CHAPTER TWO

. . . .

Tools to Get Everyone
Centered and On Track

Clearly communicating expectations to children and establishing classroom rituals will often help children anticipate what to do next. Still, having tools to help center students and bring their attention back to you is important. Perhaps it's time to start theatre class and students need an activity to help them focus on the present moment. Students who are at the beginning of an activity might need a brief activity to re-center. Or sometimes between transition periods, students who are unsure of what to do will find ways of engaging themselves. Again, they might need a brief activity to help them come back to the present moment and rejoin the theatre class. Perhaps an activity has gotten to where students aren't moving their bodies in a safe way, and they need a moment to calm down before they can proceed to the next activity or continue with the current activity. If you already have a strategy in your community to bring everyone together, you may want to continue to use that familiar and already successful strategy. This chapter contains ideas for bringing an unfocused class together, into the present moment and back into drama class. There are also breathing activities in chapter 3 that can help calm down and refocus an excited class. Use whatever works best for you and your children.

Positive Classroom Management Strategies or Centering Activities

Breathe in Unison

. . . .

Do a breathing activity to calm children's bodies and bring them into the moment. For example, a rainbow breath is where students place their hands firmly together at their chest while breathing in. While breathing out, they move their hands upward and out, like a rainbow. Do this a few times and consider allowing a student to lead the class once everyone is familiar with doing a rainbow breath. See chapter 3 for more ideas for breathing exercises.

Hum in Unison

Have everyone hum a particular note together. This helps bring the community together: when the children hear you hum, they know to join in. Wait until everyone is humming and standing still before you stop humming and continue the class.

Yoga Poses

Move into a certain yoga pose when the class needs to focus. When everyone sees you in this yoga pose, they know to get into the same pose. Try a posture-building pose, such as tree pose. It involves a lot of focus to get into this yoga pose because you are balancing on one leg. To move into a tree pose, plant your feet firmly into the earth. Raise one foot, placing it firmly on your other thigh, as high as you can. Place your hands together high over your head or at your chest. For more yoga pose ideas, see "A Yoga Story" on page 44, or consider looking at *Yoga for You and Your Child* by Mark Singleton and *Bal Yoga for Kids* by Glenda Kacev and Sylvia Roth to get ideas on how to incorporate mindfulness and yoga into your teaching practice.

Mouth Directions

Whisper, mouth silently, or act out a set of directions, such as "Stand up straight. Now put your hands down at your sides. Face forward." This gets children's attention because they have to concentrate to understand what you are trying to communicate, and it can also be humorous and engaging for the children to watch, which helps redirect their attention back to you.

Classroom Signal

Establish a signal all the children know to mean it's time to stop moving their bodies, be silent, give their full attention to you, and then do the signal with you. Wait until everyone is ready to go and doing the signal before continuing with class. The signal can be a gesture, a clapped rhythm, or a few bars of a song.

When You Hear . . .

Establish some kind of sound, whether it's made by a silly noisemaker or a meditation gong, that lets children know it's time to freeze when they hear the sound.

Actor, Neutral, Ready to Go!

This is an old favorite with theatre teachers that is very effective. *Actor neutral* is when actors put their bodies in a neutral position: their feet are grounded shoulder width apart, their arms are relaxed by their sides, their shoulders are back, and their spine is straight, as if there were a balloon holding it up. Actors are balanced with aligned posture, relaxed, and ready to work. When you want the class to focus and put their bodies in neutral, you can say, "Actor, neutral, ready to go."

1. When you say "actor," stomp down your left foot.

2. When you say "neutral," firmly stomp your right foot.

3. When you say "ready to," put out your left hand.

4. When you say "go," put out your right hand.

Repeat the activity until everyone's body is in actor neutral.

Countdown

Count down from ten. Everyone should do what you request before you reach one. For example, "Everyone should be standing in a circle by the time I reach one. 10, 9, 8, 7 . . ."

If You Are Listening

Use this game not only to bring everyone's attention back to you, but also to reflect on the themes of the day's class. For example, if the theme of the drama play session is going to the beach, you might say, "If you are listening, pretend to swim. If you are listening, dig in the sand with your hands or a toy shovel. If you are listening, listen to a seashell. If you are listening, put on sunblock." Play until everyone is together and focused.

Repeat the Rhythm

Clap a simple rhythm. Children will then repeat the rhythm back to you. Perform the same rhythm by patting your shoulders, patting your knees, or stomping your feet. Play until everyone is focused, together, and has their full attention on you.

How, Should, and Why

Ask everyone *how*, *should*, and *why* they do something before an activity starts. Here are some examples:

- Why do we have a rule that only one person speaks at a time?

- How does a good listener behave?

- Why is it important to be a good listener?

- Should we be good listeners?

- How do you feel when someone listens to you?

- How do you feel when others don't listen to you and it's your turn to speak?

Students often know what is expected of them, and sometimes they will listen to their peers better than their teachers. Also, if students don't behave as they previously stated they should, you can always remind them, "Remember how Ahmed said it's important to listen because we can't hear what people are saying if we all talk at once. I can't hear what you are saying if you all talk at once. Let's take turns." Do this in a way that is not accusatory or shaming. This is about students creating a class contract, not singling out individuals who might be making poor choices.

Turn Off the Lights

You can turn off the lights to let children know it's time to pause and give their attention to you. You can even have a small flashlight you shine on your face to bring their attention back to you.

Puppet Show Time!

Have a puppet you bring out when you want the class's attention. Perhaps the puppet has a message for the class that they won't get to hear unless they are paying attention. This can also be a great way to transition to a new activity or give students directions. Here are some scenarios that could include the puppet:

- The puppet wants to compliment kids on what they were doing well in the activity and is interrupting the class because it was so impressed with the children.

- The puppet has a question about what the children are learning about.

- The puppet needs help with something and the children, as experts, can give the puppet advice. Try to have the puppet face an issue that the children are currently facing in class or need advice on something the children are learning about. For example, if the children are learning about growing flowers and are pretending to be seeds growing into flowers in drama class, the puppet might need to consult these experts about why the flower seeds it planted in playdough won't grow.

- The puppet wants to share a funny dance or song related to today's themes with the students.

- The puppet learned a neat fact it wants to share with the class. The puppet could also be wrong and the children, as experts, may need to correct it.

- The puppet is angry, sad, or afraid, and needs a hug from each of the children or to be comforted in another way. Let the children come up with the idea of how to comfort the puppet.

PART TWO

Building a Drama Class

CHAPTER THREE

. . . .

Breathing Exercises and Techniques

Being mindful and in the present moment helps actors of all ages focus on the dramatic activities ahead. Drama class should begin with the ritual of being together in a circle and breathing together. Breathing exercises are an excellent way to start a drama class. They bring the community together as everyone shares a single breath. Breathing exercises can cultivate inner peace and help children feel calmer, relaxed, and centered. Breathing exercises can help refocus, soothe, calm, and energize the theatre troupe.

The following activities might be helpful other times during the day as well. They may help children focus and feel centered after recess or lunch. These breathing activities might help an individual who is upset and needs help calming her body.

Diaphragmatic breathing refers to deep breaths that come from the diaphragm. This type of breathing assists actors in projecting their voices over long distances so they can be heard by the audience in a large space. Proper breathing also protects actors' voices from straining. Explain to young children that diaphragmatic breaths are where their tummy expands when they inhale and goes in when they exhale.

Various Breaths

Breathing exercises are an excellent way to release tension and develop mindfulness and bodily awareness. These breaths can be practiced on their own or in the following activities. If children are practicing on their own, have participants sit in a circle facing each other, cross-legged, with their hands on their knees. The lotus pose from yoga is an excellent pose for practicing breathing, but any pose that is comfortable and relaxed works. Take a breath a few times and, once the class is familiar with doing this breathing exercise, consider allowing a student to lead the class in the breathing exercise.

Smell the Flower/Blow the Dandelion

Act it out!

1. Have actors imagine they are smelling a flower, breathing in deeply. Ask them to pretend that they are in a beautiful flower garden. Encourage them to imagine what kind of flower they are smelling, and then share with the rest of the class the type of flower they are smelling.

2. When they exhale, have them imagine that they are blowing the seeds of a dandelion.

Filling up a Balloon/Snake Breath

Act it out!

1. Tell students to imagine that as they are breathing in, they are filling a balloon inside of them.

2. When they breathe out, ask them to hiss as long and slowly as possible, like a snake or air escaping a balloon.

Wind in the Trees

Act it out!

1. Have students breathe in deeply through their noses.

2. Then students release their breath through their mouths and their teeth to make a noise like wind in the trees when they exhale.

Dragon Breath

Act it out!

1. Ask students to inhale through their noses for a count of 1, 2. Then pause.

2. Tell the children to exhale through their noses like a dragon billowing smoke for a count of 3, 4. Then repeat.

Baby Bunny Breath

Act it out!

1. Take three quick inhales through the nose, encouraging the children to imagine they are baby bunnies, sniffing the air for carrots to eat in a vegetable patch.

2. Then take one long exhale out of the nose.

Butterfly Breath

Act it out!

1. When inhaling through your mouth, raise your arms over your head, like gentle butterfly wings.

2. When exhaling, float your wings back down.

Bumblebee Breath

Act it out!

1. Breathe in through your nose.

2. Exhale through the mouth, making a faint humming sound.

Bubble Gum Breath

Act it out!

1. Have children take several deep inhales while they pantomime blowing a huge bubble, using their hands to signify the bubble getting bigger and bigger.

2. Pantomime popping the bubble.

3. Instruct children to exhale through their mouths, letting the air escape with a faint hissing sound.

Encore!

Repeat this breath several times, each time making the bubble bigger. After you pop the bubble, pantomime wiping the excess bubble gum off your legs, out of your hair, off your face, off the floor, and off your toes. The wiping action is great for developing gross-motor skills in young children.

Horse Breath

Act it out!

1. Take three short inhales through your nose.

2. Do a long exhale, blowing your lips like a horse.

Yawn!

Act it out!

1. Take several deep yawns.

2. Stretch your arms upward with each yawn.

Silly Face Breath

Act it out!

1. Have children stick out their tongues and stretch their faces out as wide as they can.

2. Remind them to take deep breaths in and out.

Rainbow Breath

Act it out!

1. Children place hands firmly together at their chest while breathing in.

2. While breathing out, they move their hands upward and out, like a rainbow.

One-Nostril Breath

Act it out!

1. Put two fingers on the side of one nostril and close your mouth.

2. Breathe in deeply through the open nostril.

3. Breathe out through your mouth like you are blowing out a candle on a birthday cake.

4. Do this several times, then switch and practice breathing out of the other nostril.

Ha! Ha! Ho! Ho!

Act it out!

1. Repeat various sounds on a different short breath each time you say the sound.

2. Say each sound at least five times in a row before moving on to the next sound. Some sounds to start with are:

   • ha

   • ho

   • he

Big Balloon

Act it out!

1. Tell students to imagine they are blowing up a huge balloon. Take multiple, huge deep breaths to fill up the balloon.

2. Use your hands to show how big their balloons are, and how much it is growing each time you blow. Have students show how big their balloons are with their hands.

3. Pantomime releasing the imaginary balloon and make the sound of the air escaping the balloon by exhaling through your teeth, making a sort of hissing sound. You can even point to where your imaginary balloon flew off to.

Breathing Exercises

Lift the Beanbag

Materials

o small beanbag animals or small beanbags, one for each student

Act it out!

1. Ask the students to lie on their backs.

2. Place a small beanbag animal or beanbag on the stomach of each student.

3. Have the children practice diaphragmatic breathing, taking deep breaths that fill their lungs, like a balloon, and lift the beanbag up, then exhaling, letting the beanbag come back down.

Spotlight on . . .
COGNITIVE
DEVELOPMENT

1, 2, 3, Repeat after Me!

Act it out!

1. Have actors sit in a circle.

2. Say, "1, 2, 3, repeat after me," and then demonstrate a breath, such as one big breath through the nose and three short breaths through the mouth.

3. Say, "Now you try." See if the class can repeat the way you were breathing.

Encore!

Do this activity using the various breaths listed above, or have the actors create breaths that the rest of the class can do.

Spotlight on . . .
COGNITIVE
DEVELOPMENT

Pinwheel Breath

Materials

o pinwheels, one for each student

Act it out!

1. Have students sit in a circle.

2. Practice taking a few deep diaphragmatic breaths with the children, where their tummies expand when they inhale and go in when they exhale. Have them place their hands on their tummies so they can feel the air coming in and expanding their diaphragms when they inhale and going out when they exhale.

3. Give each student a pinwheel.

4. Have the class practice taking long breaths in and out. When the children exhale, they should breathe out onto their pinwheel, making it spin.

5. Allow children to see how long they can exhale. Have them try to exhale longer each time. See if they can exhale for two seconds, then three seconds, then four seconds, then five seconds. Count using your fingers held up in the air so children can see how many seconds they have spent exhaling.

Spotlight on . . .
COGNITIVE
DEVELOPMENT

Fill the Bowl

Materials

o plastic bowls, two for each child

o small squares of paper, enough for each child

o straws, one for each child

Act it out!

1. Cut out small scraps of paper and place them around an empty bowl. Provide two empty bowls for each child. Make sure children have enough space to work without bumping heads with another participant.

2. Using a big inhale, children use the straws to suck up the small squares of paper from one bowl and carry them into the other bowl before exhaling and dropping the paper into the other bowl.

Encore!

Children can also use this method of moving paper to create a beautiful collage by dropping pieces onto a sheet of sticky contact paper or a piece of construction paper covered with glue.

Spotlight on . . .
CREATIVITY
& THE ARTS

PHYSICAL & MOTOR
DEVELOPMENT

Blowing Feathers

Materials

- feathers, one for each child

Act it out!

1. Have the children sit in a circle facing one another.

2. Give each child a feather.

3. Holding the feathers in front of their faces, the students can practice inhaling and exhaling. When they breathe out, their feathers will move slightly.

Encore!

Let children blow their feathers across a smooth surface like a table. They can even have a feather-blowing race or dance party with music.

Bubble Blowing

Materials

- bubble mixture
- bubble blowers, one per student

Act it out!

1. Give each child a bubble blower.

2. Have the children practice taking deep diaphragmatic breaths, letting their tummies come out like a bubble whenever they breathe in.

3. Once they have practiced deep breaths, allow them to blow bubbles using these deep breaths.

Spotlight on . . .
PHYSICAL & MOTOR
DEVELOPMENT

Spotlight on . . .
PHYSICAL & MOTOR
DEVELOPMENT

CHAPTER FOUR

· ·

Vocal Warm-ups

The voice is an important tool for actors. Actors need their voices to project to fill the space if performing inside, or over long distances if performing outside, so that everyone in the audience can hear them. Actors need to speak clearly and use good diction to be understood by the audience, who may be seated far away or in places with poor acoustics. Actors must disguise their voices so they can play different characters, such as an elderly person or a tiny mouse. And actors also use their voices to express different emotions.

Vocal warm-ups allow young children to use their voices in creative and expressive ways. It's a space to use their voices in different ways than they might be accustomed to. Vocal exercises also warm up the voice to prevent strain on the vocal chords, as children may be using their voices during drama class in uncustomary ways, such as creating sound effects, singing, or projecting loudly.

Vocal Warm-up Activities

Laugh like a . . .

. . . .

Act it out!

1. Stand in a circle as a class.

2. All of you will laugh together like different people or animals.

3. You will conduct, so when your hands are up high in the air, everyone is their loudest; when your hands are down low, everyone gets softer as your hands get closer to the floor. When your hands are touching the floor, everyone is silent.

Encore!

Here are some different characters or animals you can laugh as:

- a hyena
- Santa Claus
- a wicked witch
- a tiny baby
- an old man
- a teeny tiny mouse

- an enormous, huge giant
- a bear
- a chicken
- a duck
- the Count from Sesame Street

Spotlight on . . .
PHYSICAL & MOTOR
DEVELOPMENT

SOCIAL & EMOTIONAL
LEARNING

Who Is It?

. . . .

Materials

o a bandana

o a chair

Act it out!

1. Have one child sit in a chair and tie a bandana over her eyes.

2. Have the rest of the class line up behind the child in the chair.

3. The child in the chair will ask, "Who is it?"

4. The child at the front of the line will disguise his voice and say a silly made-up name.

5. The child in the chair will try to guess whose voice it is. If she doesn't guess who the voice belongs to, that child can tell her who he is.

6. Let everyone in the class try to fool the person sitting in the chair.

7. Then allow another person to sit in the chair and let the game continue.

Spotlight on . . .
SOCIAL & EMOTIONAL
LEARNING

Act it out!

1. Have students stand in a circle.

2. Name an emotion, then go around the circle and have everyone say, "Really?!" one at a time using that emotion.

3. Each time around the circle, you will give a new emotion. Here are some emotions you can name to have the children say "Really?!":

   - excited
   - sad
   - angry
   - tired
   - confused
   - bored
   - jealous/envious
   - hungry

Encore!

You can also use other phrases or words that relate to what the children are learning in another area. For example, if it's Halloween, you might have them say, "Boo" or "Trick or treat" with different emotions.

If students are too nervous to talk alone, have the group say the phrases together. Encourage the students to gesture or move.

You can also describe a situation that would create that emotion: for example, "You are angry like someone just stole your favorite toy and won't give it back." Or "You are sad like you have to leave a friend's house and you want to play more."

Ask the class for emotions or situations where they have felt a strong emotion.

Spotlight on . . .
SOCIAL & EMOTIONAL
LEARNING

Now You Try!

Materials

o various sound effects and wacky noises (there are many websites that contain free audio samples of sound effects you can play)

Act it out!

1. Play a sound effect or a wacky noise for the class.

2. See if students can mimic the sound with their voices.

3. Try different sound effects or wacky noises, playing each one at a time.

Spotlight on . . .
COGNITIVE
DEVELOPMENT

Materials

o individual pieces of paper or notecards with various images on them, such as the following:

• a car

• a cow

• a chicken

• a person sleeping

• a duck

• a dog

• a tea kettle boiling

Act it out!

1. Have children stand or sit in a circle.

2. Show them one card at a time, and see if, as a group or individually, they can create the sound associated with the image on the card.

Encore!

Tell a story using the different sounds and use the cards to let the class know when to make certain sound effects.

Spotlight on . . .
APPROACHES TO
LEARNING

Create a Voice

Materials

o a huge bag of various stuffed animals

Act it out!

1. Instruct the class to sit in a circle on the floor.

2. One at a time, let each student pull out a stuffed animal from your huge bag.

3. Have each child create a silly voice for the stuffed animal they pulled from the bag.

4. Ask the stuffed animal a question such as "What is your name?" or "How are you?"

5. The student responds as the stuffed animal using his silly voice.

6. Have the class ask the stuffed animal a question or two before moving on to the next student.

Spotlight on . . .
SOCIAL & EMOTIONAL
LEARNING

Encore!

Encourage the children to move their stuffed animals as they would puppets.

This is a great activity to use if students have made a puppet or are working with puppets.

Jungle Orchestra

Act it out!

1. Divide the students into groups of two or three.

2. Assign each group a different animal. Here are some examples of animals you can assign children:

   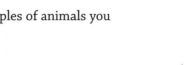

   • elephants

   • lions

   • monkeys

   • snakes

3. You will act as the "conductor" for the jungle orchestra. When your hands are up high, the children can make their animals' noises get louder. When your hands are down low, the animal noises are softer. Have a signal for when students should be silent.

4. Practice with the different sections.

Spotlight on . . .
CREATIVITY &
THE ARTS

Number Echo

Act it out!

1. Say a number using various voices and pitches—high, low, silly, or scary.

2. Have the children repeat back the number using the same inflection.

3. Let the children take turns saying the number in a silly voice that the class tries to mimic.

Encore!

You can also do this activity using letters in the alphabet.

Spotlight on . . .
APPROACHES TO
LEARNING

Create a Rainstorm

Act it out!

1. Start by blowing through your teeth, making the sound of the wind.

2. Snap your fingers; the rain is starting!

3. Pound on your lap; the rain is falling harder!

4. Pound on the floor with your feet and make the sound of thunder with your voices. It's become a thunderstorm!

5. Pound on your lap; the rainstorm is getting lighter.

6. Snap your fingers; the rainstorm is lessening.

7. Whistle or cheep like birds chirping; the storm is finally over!

Spotlight on . . .
CREATIVITY &
THE ARTS

Act it out!

1. Have 4–6 children sit in a row.

2. One child will be the conductor. (You may need to be the conductor first, to demonstrate the game.)

3. The seated children are the musicians and will each create a sound effect that they will repeat. The sound effect can be as simple as a student clapping the same rhythm or singing a single note. Each child's sound effect should be different.

4. When the conductor gently touches a musician's head, the musician is allowed to start making her noise. When the conductor gently touches the musician's head again, the musician will have to stop making noise. The conductor can have all musicians playing at once or one playing at a time.

5. If the conductor wants the group to get louder, the conductor should raise his hands high. If he wants them to play softer, he should put his hands to the ground.

6. Let each child have a turn as a conductor and as the instruments.

Encore!

Here are some themes and ideas for sounds the children can make:

On the pond:

duck quacking

baby duck quacking

frog ribbitting

fish (gulping sound)

In the barnyard:

pig oinking

cow mooing

horse neighing

chicken clucking

sheep baaing

baby animal
(calf, sheep,
piglet, etc.)

In the meadow:

birds chirping

bees buzzing

At nighttime:

wolf howling

owl hooting

crickets chirping

On Halloween:

witch cackling

wind blowing eerily

ghostly moaning

wolf howling

evil laughter

Materials

- a sack or pillowcase full of different toy cars, trains, planes, and other modes of transportation

Act it out!

1. Have children sit in a circle.

2. One at a time, let each child pull a toy out of the bag.

3. Ask the child to make the sound of the toy.

4. Afterward, invite the entire class to make the sound of the toy.

5. Put the toy back inside the bag or set it aside (depending on if you have enough for each child to select a different toy) and let the next child pull out a toy.

Encore!

You can also do this game using farm animal figurines.

Spotlight on . . .
CREATIVITY &
THE ARTS

A Cuddly Talk Show

Materials

- two chairs

- favorite stuffed animals (ask children to bring one from home ahead of time, but also have extras in case a child forgets)

Act it out!

1. Place two chairs in front of the class and instruct the children to be a live television audience, sitting in rows in front of the chairs.

2. The talk show host (you) and the guest (the student and his stuffed animal) will sit in the two chairs.

3. You will interview the student's favorite toy as a flamboyant television host! The student will respond as his stuffed animal.

4. Make sure to involve the audience by asking them for questions or asking them to give a warm applause to each guest.

5. Have each student come up one at a time to be the voice of the stuffed animal being interviewed.

Spotlight on . . .
CREATIVITY &
THE ARTS

Materials

o a large stuffed animal (such as an elephant)

Act it out!

This activity is great if you are teaching children how to project their voices for the stage.

1. Explain to the class that onstage, actors need to speak loudly enough so that those seated far away can hear them. Have students sit in a line at one end of the classroom. Place a huge stuffed animal, such as a huge elephant named Ms. Elephant, at the opposite end of the classroom.

2. Have a child say, "Hello, Ms. Elephant!" to the huge stuffed animal. If she is projecting her voice loudly enough, have her come over and give Ms. Elephant a hug. After she has given Ms. Elephant a hug, she can then sit down next to Ms. Elephant.

3. Invite the next student to say, "Hello, Ms. Elephant!" Let the students sitting next to Ms. Elephant tell the projecting student whether or not they can hear him.

4. Play until all the children have had the opportunity to say hello to Ms. Elephant and practiced projecting their voices.

Encore!

Try again, except this time move Ms. Elephant even farther away.

If students are very shy, they can pass or try to beat their personal best.

Spotlight on . . .
CREATIVITY &
THE ARTS

Pass the Sound

Act it out!

1. Have actors sit in a circle.

2. One actor begins by making a sound.

3. The next child tries to make the exact same sound.

4. Pass the sound around the entire circle.

5. Let the child seated next to the person who started the first sound begin the next sound.

Spotlight on . . .
CREATIVITY &
THE ARTS

CHAPTER FIVE

. . . .

Warm-ups for the Mind and Body

Warm-ups are short activities that prepare the body, heart, and mind for drama class. Warm-ups are a vital part of any drama class: they prepare the body physically for movement. Concentration, focus, and listening activities lead the mind into the exciting, nurturing, and exploratory space of that day's drama activities. They prepare the heart for the safe, supportive, and warm space of the classroom's culture and for empathetic engagement. Warm-ups also provide the students with the emotional timbre of the day's journey. These brief activities set the tone and create the world that young actors will be exploring and playing in.

Concentration, Focus, and Listening Warm-up Activities

Professional actors must be focused when performing. They are responding to the verbal and nonverbal cues of other actors to shape their performance. They are fully present in the world of the play they are performing in.

Young children benefit from doing concentration and focus activities as part of their drama class warm-up. These activities help clear their minds and focus their energy into drama class. These activities also help direct their energy into the present moment and one another.

These concentration, focus, and listening activities might be useful at other times throughout the day as well. Perhaps before you start an art activity, your class can do a focus activity together. Maybe after recess, if children are having trouble transitioning into a more sedentary activity like music class, you can use a concentration activity to help them re-center. A listening activity might be helpful before you give a demonstration or directions, such as showing them how to plant a seed.

Circle Stretch

· ·

Act it out!

1. Have the class stand in a circle with their arms extended, fingers touching their neighbors'. This stretches the body and puts students a safe distance apart to start doing drama activities.

What's the Difference?

· ·

Act it out!

1. Have children get into pairs.

2. One child turns around, closes his eyes, and counts to ten, while the other changes something about her appearance, such as untucking her shirt, putting her hair down, or rolling down a sock.

3. When the counter has reached ten, he opens his eyes, turns around, and tries to guess what the partner changed.

Big Tree! Little Tree!

· ·

Act it out!

1. Have children stand in a circle.

2. Demonstrate the actions for big tree and little tree for the children. When you say "big tree," spread your body out as tall and big as you can. When you say "little tree," make your body as small as you can. Perform the actions together as a group. Say "big tree" and "little tree" together.

3. Go around the circle. One child will say "big tree" while completing the action; then the next child will say "little tree" while doing the action.

Encore!

See how fast you can go around the circle.

You can also perform this warm-up as big fish, little fish. Hold your arms out wide for big fish or teeny tiny for little fish.

You can also create a pattern that the group must adhere to, such as three big trees and one little tree, to teach students about creating patterns.

On the Beach! In the Ocean!

Act it out!

1. Have the children stand in a line side by side.

2. Tell them to close their eyes and imagine they are on the shore of a beach. The waves of the ocean are in front of them.

3. Instruct children to open their eyes. When you say "in the ocean," the children jump forward one hop like they are jumping into the waves. When you say "on the beach," they jump backward one hop.

4. Say "on the beach" and "in the ocean" at various speeds. Sometimes say "on the beach" or "in the ocean" twice in a row to make sure the students are listening.

5. Congratulate the children for being good listeners.

Spotlight on . . .
PHYSICAL & MOTOR
DEVELOPMENT

Count Down and Up

Materials

o a ball

Act it out!

1. Have actors stand in a circle.

2. The child who starts with the ball says "one" and then throws the ball to another child.

3. When each child catches the ball, he says the next number. Play until ten, or until every child has had a turn. If a child does not know a number, she just needs to ask and a classmate can tell her.

Encore!

You can also do this activity with the alphabet.

Children can count up or down.

You can play to see how high children can count or aim to reach a specific number, such as ten.

You can play with speed, having the children go fast or slow.

Children can count softly or loudly, or they can increase their volume as the numbers get higher.

Spotlight on . . .
PHYSICAL & MOTOR
DEVELOPMENT

SOCIAL & EMOTIONAL
LEARNING

Act it out!

1. Have students sit across from a partner. One actor will be the mirror, the other will be the person looking in.

2. The actor looking at the "mirror" will strike a pose. The mirror partner will copy the pose exactly. Tell the actors when to make a pose by saying "3, 2, 1, action."

3. After each pose, the actors switch roles.

Encore!

Students can also play this game by slowly copying each other's movements. Partners must work together to fool the teacher, who is trying to guess which partner is the mirror and which is the actor.

Spotlight on . . .
SOCIAL & EMOTIONAL
LEARNING

PHYSICAL & MOTOR
DEVELOPMENT

Countdown

Act it out!

1. Tell students to stand in a circle.

2. The students count to ten. Beginning at one, they will be as quiet and as low to the ground as they can be. By ten, they will be as big and loud as they can be.

3. The class then counts back down to one, getting gradually softer.

Spotlight on . . .
SOCIAL & EMOTIONAL
LEARNING

Pass the Kitty

Materials

○ a stuffed animal

Act it out!

1. Have children sit in a circle facing each other. Provide a small stuffed animal (any will work), such as a kitten.

2. One student will sit in the center of the circle with his eyes closed.

3. Count to ten or sing the alphabet song as a class while the children pass the stuffed animal around the circle behind their backs.

4. When you reach ten or the end of the song, the child in the center will open his eyes. All the other children keep their hands behind their backs.

5. The child in the center will have three guesses to decide who has the kitty behind her back. If the child doesn't guess correctly after three tries, the student holding the stuffed animal will reveal the stuffed animal.

6. The child who had the stuffed animal behind her back will be the next to go in the center.

Spotlight on . . .
SOCIAL & EMOTIONAL
LEARNING

Act it out!

1. Instruct the children to stand or sit in a circle or in a straight line facing you.

2. Carefully model for the children how to create each fingerplay you will use at the beginning of the game. Consider using only a few actions that relate to the day's theme so as not to confuse the students.

3. You will call out different directions. When you call out "left" or "right," children must move their hands left or right, shaking them like "jazz hands." Let the students practice moving their hands left and right.

4. When you call out a fingerplay, such as "butterfly," the class must act out the fingerplay with their hands. Fingerplays might include the following:

   • butterfly (put thumbs together and move fingers like the wings of a butterfly)

   • wiggle fingers (wiggle fingers in front of the body)

   • touch the earth (reach hands down to the ground)

   • reach for the sky (reach hands up toward the sky)

   • make a spider (put hands together and move them as though the fingers are the legs of a spider)

   • move your hands in circles (rotate hands at the wrist)

   • rock (make a fist)

   • clap (clap hands together)

   • asleep (put hands together and rest your head on them)

   If the class is learning about the weather, a fingerplay might include these ideas:

   • rainy (fingers moving downward and wiggling like raindrops falling)

   • windy (fingers moving side to side like they are tree branches blowing in the wind)

   • sunny (fingers radiating around each child's face as she smiles)

   • snowy (fingers drifting downward like snowflakes)

5. Here is an example of how to call out actions: "Left. Right. Left. Right. Left. Right. Butterfly. Left. Right. Spider. Rock. Left. Right. Circles. Left. Right. Left. Right. Butterfly. Butterfly. Touch the sky. Touch the earth. Touch the sky. Touch the earth. Rock. Butterfly. Spider. Left. Right. Left. Right."

Encore!

If the class has extra energy, the children can do this game while standing. Have them run left and right each time you say "left" or "right." Instead of fingerplays, you can create actions students perform with their entire bodies, such as butterfly wings with their arms. Complete all the whole-body actions while standing in place.

Spotlight on . . .
PHYSICAL & MOTOR
DEVELOPMENT

Materials

o yoga mats, one per child

Act it out!

Basic yoga is a fantastic way to start a drama class. The three parts of yoga—meditation, breathing, and exercise—have a host of benefits for young children. Physically, yoga develops kinesthetic intelligence by improving bodily awareness, posture, alignment, balance, coordination, and flexibility. Psychologically, yoga helps young children relax, be in the present, clear their minds, self-regulate, and self-soothe. Yoga can promote a positive body image and increase confidence. Doing yoga as a community can connect the class and help the group focus and calm down.

Below is a list of poses that you can do with students to help get their bodies warmed up and their minds and hearts engaged. Again, consider looking at *Bal Yoga for Kids* by Glenda Kacev and Sylvia Roth to get more ideas of yoga poses you can do.

1. Create and tell a story that involves all the different poses.

2. Encourage students to imagine themselves as being the different poses. For example, be a strong, tall, mountain; a beautiful, leafy tree; or a slippery, slithering cobra in the grass.

3. The story may sound like this: "Once, on a strong, tall mountain . . . let's make a tall mountain with our bodies, our feet firmly planted in the earth. Take a deep breath in, like you are smelling a flower, like you are blowing on a dandelion. And another deep breath of that crisp mountain air. Now, on this tall mountain, a slippery, slithering cobra went past a beautiful, leafy tree. Let's make a slippery, slithering cobra."

Encore!

Some yoga poses to try include the following:

Mountain Pose: Your feet are firmly planted on the ground, your spine is long and aligned, your shoulders are rolled back, and your palms are pressed together as you take deep breaths.

Child's Pose: The knees tuck underneath your body and your forehead rests on the earth. Your arms can be down at your sides or stretched out long in front of you, palms to the earth.

Forward Fold and Rag Doll Pose: Your feet are planted firmly on the earth. Bend over, letting your body hang into a forward fold, hands touching the earth. Then, grasp your elbows with your hands to move into the rag doll pose.

Tree Pose: Plant your feet firmly into the earth. Raise one foot, placing it firmly on your other thigh, as high as you can. Place hands together high over your head or at your chest.

Happy Baby Pose: Lie on your back with your legs bent and your hands holding your feet, moving like a happy baby.

Downward Dog: Your palms and feet are firmly planted into the earth with your hips raised toward the sky.

Cobra: Lay facedown on the ground with your legs and feet extended back. Pushing your palms into the earth, gently lift up your torso. Keep your lower body on the floor.

Remind children to take deep, mindful breaths. Breathing is an important part of their yoga practice.

There are many picture books that contain excellent yoga stories, such as *Good Morning Yoga* or *Good Night Yoga* by Mariam Gates.

Spotlight on . . .
PHYSICAL & MOTOR
DEVELOPMENT

COGNITIVE
DEVELOPMENT

Pass the Shape
. . . .

Materials

○ pictures of various shapes (square, circle, rectangle, and triangle) displayed somewhere visible to students such as on a poster, chalkboard, or smartboard

Act it out!

1. Pair each actor with a partner.

2. Have one actor use her finger to draw a shape on her partner's back.

3. The other actor has to try to guess what the shape is.

4. Take turns.

Encore!

You can also play this game in a line. Try to pass the shape down the line so the last person guesses what shape it is.

You can play this game by drawing letters or numbers as well.

Familiar Favorites

Here are some classic children's games that can also be used during a drama play session warm-up to nurture focus.

Who Is the Leader?
. . . .

Act it out!

1. Have the group sit cross-legged in a circle.

2. Select one child to be the guesser. The guesser will go out of sight and sound of the group.

3. You will pick a child to be the leader. Staying seated, the leader will lead the class through clapping, snapping, stomping, or patting on his lap. Everyone else will follow the leader's movements.

4. When the guesser returns to the group, she will have three tries to guess who is the leader. If she hasn't guessed in three turns, the leader reveals himself. The person who was the leader becomes the guesser for the next round.

Encore!

You can also play this game standing in a circle or moving freely around the room, following the actions of the designated leader.

Materials

o bandana to cover the cat's eyes, if necessary

o four chairs

Act it out!

This game is based on the classic children's game four corners.

1. Set up four chairs, one in each corner of the room.

2. One child is the cat in the center of the room. The other children are mice.

3. The cat counts to ten with her eyes closed or covered with a bandana. The mice tiptoe silently to a different chair in the room. No one can stay in the same corner that they were in when the cat first started counting.

4. With her eyes still closed, the cat guesses which corner the most mice are in, based on what she can hear. The mice in the loudest corner are caught. Of the mice that were caught, one of them will be the new cat.

5. Play until everyone who wants to has an opportunity to be the cat or until everyone is emotionally ready to move on.

Quietest Mouse!

Act it out!

1. Have the children scurry around the room as mice.

2. Ignite their imaginations by asking them questions about what it is like to be a mouse. How could a mouse move? What might mice like? What would mice be afraid of? What would a mouse be doing? The mice would be quiet so they could avoid the cat and sneak away with cheese or crumbs.

3. Choose the quietest child. This little mouse is the "quietest mouse."

4. Let that child choose the next quietest mouse.

5. Then the next child chosen will choose someone else to be the quietest mouse, out of the children who haven't been chosen yet.

6. Play until every child has had a chance to be the "quietest mouse" or until everyone is emotionally ready to move on.

Encore!

You can also play this game if you are waiting in a hallway or other area.

Spotlight on . . .
PHYSICAL & MOTOR
DEVELOPMENT

Spotlight on . . .
SOCIAL & EMOTIONAL
LEARNING

Spotlight on . . .
SOCIAL & EMOTIONAL
LEARNING

Telephone

Act it out!

1. The children sit in a circle.

2. Either a child or the teacher whispers a phrase to one child.

3. The child whispers the phrase to the child next to him, and then that child whispers it to the child next to her, on around the circle.

4. See if the last person can guess what the phrase is. If he guesses incorrectly, go around the circle and have each person repeat what they heard. Find out where the phrase lost its original meaning.

Encore!

Try to whisper phrases related to the day's theme. For example, if the class is learning about the rain forest, then whisper a short, neat fact about the rain forest.

One-Word Story

Materials

○ beanbag or small toy (optional)

Act it out!

1. All the actors sit in a circle.

2. They tell a story one word at a time. You can even give the children an object to pass, like a beanbag or small toy for the designated speaker to hold, so they remember that only one person speaks at a time.

3. The actors can add punctuation like a period, question mark, or exclamation point, but it's not necessary.

Encore!

Write down the story and dramatically read it aloud, letting children do the sound effects.

Children can illustrate the story afterward, drawing a moment in the story, a character, or how the story made them feel.

The class can create a short skit based off the story.

Create a picture book as a class, having each child draw a different moment in the story. Read the book together after all the children have finished illustrating their pictures.

Spotlight on . . .
SOCIAL & EMOTIONAL
LEARNING

Balloon Bounce!

Materials

o one or more balloons

Act it out!

1. Have children sit or stand in a circle.

2. Throw one balloon into the circle and see how
   long the students can keep it up in the air.

3. Add more balloons slowly. See how many balloons
   they can keep up in the air.

Encore!

You can do this activity using only a single body part, like elbows or heads, to
add an extra degree of challenge.

The class can also count how many times the group can keep the balloon up in
the air before it touches the ground.

Spotlight on . . .
COGNITIVE
DEVELOPMENT

A Name Game: Snap, Clap, Pat

Act it out!

Here is a fun way to get to know the names of the students in your class.

1. Have actors sit in a circle.

2. One actor starts by saying her name and either snapping, clapping her hands,
   or patting somewhere on her body, like her head or tummy.

3. The next child says the name and does the actions of the previous person,
   followed by adding his name and action. Have the group say the names and
   complete the actions of each classmate so they are engaged the whole time.
   If it's too complicated for children to repeat the names and actions of those
   before them, then just do the children's names one at a time without repeating
   the others.

Encore!

If this game seems too complicated for your children, offer only two options,
like clapping or patting their heads.

Spotlight on . . .
COGNITIVE
DEVELOPMENT
SOCIAL & EMOTIONAL
LEARNING

Energizing Warm-up Activities

Energizing warm-ups are excellent for a variety of circumstances. They help children become engaged at the beginning of a drama lesson and warm up their bodies. Physically vigorous activities can help children who are tired or sluggish become engaged in the drama class. Energizing warm-ups can be used throughout the day as well: One of these activities can be employed when children need the opportunity to move in a structured and fun way after doing a stationary activity. One of these activities might be suitable while children are waiting during a transition and need something fun to keep them occupied and moving safely. These activities are a wonderful opportunity for students to let loose and have fun together in a safe and structured way. You can employ these activities indoors or outdoors.

Time to Say Hello!

Materials

o music

Act it out!

1. Play the music and allow actors to move freely around the space, saying hello to one another.

2. Everyone freezes when you stop the music.

3. Wait until everyone is frozen before you share a new way for everyone to say hello.

4. Play the music again when it is time for the children to move freely.

5. Encourage the actors to come up with the different ways of saying hello. They could say hello with actions like these:

- giving high fives
- offering a handshake
- whispering secretively
- dancing
- using American Sign Language
- saying hello in different languages
- bowing or curtsying
- pretending to be various animals
- saluting each other

- waving
- fist bumping
- smiling
- pretending to be characters from a book or movie the class enjoys
- telling your classmate one thing you like or appreciate about him
- giving an imaginary gift—students can decide what gift they are giving

Spotlight on . . .
CREATIVITY &
THE ARTS

PHYSICAL & MOTOR
DEVELOPMENT

Materials

o a beanbag, soft ball, or beanbag animal

Act it out!

1. Give the group a category such as the following:

   • fruit   • furniture   • candy bars   • shapes

   • sports   • dinosaurs   • colors

2. After you give the group a category, name something in that category, such as "Types of vegetables, carrots."

3. Throw the beanbag to someone else in the group. That person must say something in that category, such as "green beans." Children cannot say something someone else said already, so they need to pay attention. If they can't think of something in that category that hasn't been said, they can ask a friend to help them.

4. See if the group can get at least ten different items in each category before moving on to a new category.

Spotlight on . . .
COGNITIVE
DEVELOPMENT

APPROACHES TO
LEARNING

Good Morning! Let's . . .

Act it out!

1. Have children stand in a circle.

2. Explain that *pantomime* means acting out doing something without speech, using only gestures.

3. Say, "Good morning! Let's . . ." and then pantomime an activity you might do in the morning as a class, such as stretch awake.

4. Go to the next person and have him say, "Good morning! Let's . . ." and pantomime stretching awake, and then add a new activity, such as brushing his teeth.

5. Go around the circle, adding something new each time. You can do all the previous activities each time or just the new activity, depending on the group's size and abilities.

Spotlight on . . .
PHYSICAL & MOTOR
DEVELOPMENT

Act it out!

1. Have students stand in a circle.

2. Say, "On your mark, get set . . ."

3. List an action for the children to perform, such as:

   - run in place
   - flap your wings like a chicken
   - blow a huge imaginary balloon
   - jump in place like a kangaroo
   - be an airplane, standing in place
   - touch the sky

   - touch the ground
   - shake out everything
   - wobble like you are stuck in a big bowl of Jell-O
   - dance in place
   - make a silly face

4. Say, "Freeze!" when it's time for students to move on to the next activity. When everyone is standing still, say, "On your mark, get set . . ." before giving them the next action.

Abracadabra! The Silly Wizard

Materials

- a wizard's hat (optional)

Act it out!

1. Have students stand in a circle.

2. One student stands in the middle of the circle and is "the silly wizard." The silly wizard can wear a goofy wizard's hat. You should be the first silly wizard. You will move around the circle, attempting to make another student smile or laugh with a silly trick or made-up magic spell.

3. If the silly wizard standing in the circle can say "abracadabra" without smiling or laughing, she keeps her spot in the circle. If the other student smiles or laughs, he enters the circle and becomes the silly wizard, donning the hat and trying to make the others laugh.

Director's note

Remind children not to touch their classmates or enter others' space when attempting to make their friends smile or laugh. If someone is uncomfortable being in the center or has been the silly wizard for a while, find a volunteer who hasn't been the silly wizard yet and wants to be, or volunteer yourself to be the silly wizard in the middle.

Act it out!

1. Ask the actors to sit in a circle facing each other.

2. Have the children cover their faces with their hands. Tell them what type of emotion mask they will be "wearing" with their facial expressions when they remove their hands. Don't be afraid to demonstrate this for them several times until they are comfortable and understand the game. Explain each emotion mask briefly, or ask a volunteer to explain, to make sure everyone understands what the emotion is.

3. After viewing the various masks the actors have "put on," ask the children to raise their hands if they have ever felt this feeling before.

4. If time allows, invite the students to share times when they have felt like a certain emotion mask. Let them know that every emotion is natural and healthy.

Encore!

When you remove your hands, your emotion mask will be:

• angry	• nervous	• sad	• silly
• brave	• proud	• shy	• sleepy
• confused			• stubborn
• excited			• surprised
• happy			

Spotlight on . . .
SOCIAL & EMOTIONAL
LEARNING

I Like To . . .

Act it out!

1. Have actors stand in a circle.

2. Pantomime several activities you like to do, such as reading, singing, dancing, painting, playing an instrument.

3. Going around the circle, each actor will say his name and pantomime something he likes to do. After each child shares his pantomime, the students can act out as a group what that person likes doing.

4. Finally, have the children raise their hands, then touch their toes, then wiggle all over if they enjoy doing the activity their classmate likes to do.

Spotlight on . . .
CREATIVITY &
THE ARTS

How Are You Feeling?

Act it out!

1. Ask students to stand in a circle. Share with them how you are feeling (for example, "I am feeling excited!"). Remind them there is no right or wrong answer; they should be honest.

2. Take turns going around the circle to ask each child how she is feeling.

3. Invite the group to make a face, perform a gesture, or move their bodies into a posture to reflect that feeling.

Chewing Bubble Gum

Act it out!

1. Students will exercise their facial muscles by chewing an imaginary piece of gum.

2. Chew to the left, right, fast and slow, and even blow a bubble.

Today for Lunch . . .

Act it out!

1. Ask the students to sit in a circle.

2. Instruct the children to pantomime making and eating various foods. For example, if a child was making a peanut butter and jelly sandwich, she would act out opening and closing the bread bag, opening the peanut butter jar and jelly jar, then spreading on the peanut butter and jelly.

3. Ask the class various questions to expand the drama activity. What would they like to prepare for lunch? What are their favorite types of food? What did they eat for lunch? What would be a healthy lunch?

4. Today for lunch, we will . . .

   • drink a glass of water

   • eat grapes

   • eat a peanut butter sandwich

   • eat carrots dipped in hummus

   • eat a banana

   • eat an ice cream cone for dessert

   • do the dishes and wipe down the table

You can choose any meal or base it on what time of day it is.

Materials

o music (recommended)

Act it out!

1. Clear the classroom space or play outside in an open area. Line up the children along a wall, not in front of each other but spread out evenly.

2. Instruct the students in how to cross the classroom using different movements. Turn on music to help create a fun and engaging environment.

3. Once the children reach the wall on the other side, they should wait for instructions about the next movement they will use to cross the classroom. Allow students to offer suggestions. Here are ideas for different movements the class could perform to cross the room:

- jumping
- marching
- crawling
- hopping
- swimming
- galloping
- dancing
- tiptoeing
- ballet dancing
- dribbling an imaginary basketball
- jumping an imaginary jump rope

- like they're on the moon
- as robots
- as various animals
- using teeny tiny steps
- in slow motion
- as if the floor were covered in Jell-O
- as if the floor were covered in ice
- as if the floor were covered in deep mud
- as if the floor were covered in sticky glue

Director's note

Sometimes students want to run. Say, "I can see that you find running fun, and drama should be fun, but I want us all to be safe and not run into each other or fall down and get hurt. That's why we don't run in drama class. You can run outside during playtime. Now, that was a great idea! What is another great idea for how we can cross the room?" Validating young actors by letting them know their request is great but not ideal for this environment is an important way of supporting them and keeping them engaged while not allowing choices that might not be safe for that space.

Spotlight on . . .
PHYSICAL & MOTOR
DEVELOPMENT

CREATIVITY &
THE ARTS

Spotlight on . . .
PHYSICAL & MOTOR
DEVELOPMENT

Act it out!

1. Actors can work together in pairs, in small groups, or as a large group.

2. Have actors create various shapes using different parts of their bodies.

3. Encourage the children to work together to create the various shapes, such as four actors lying down to make a square or rectangle, or perhaps an actor creating a triangle with a partner using their arms.

Familiar Favorites

Here are some games you might already be familiar with that are excellent for warming up the body.

We're Gonna . . .

· ·

Act it out!

1. Have all participants stand in a circle.

2. You can do this shakedown with different body parts using the lyrics below. You can sing or say the words.

> We're gonna shake, shake, shake, shake, shake our hands
> We're gonna shake, shake, shake, shake, shake our hands
> We're gonna shake, shake, shake, shake, shake our hands
> We're gonna shake, shake, shake, shake, shake our hands
>
> We're gonna shake, shake, shake, shake, shake our feet
> We're gonna shake, shake, shake, shake, shake our feet
> We're gonna shake, shake, shake, shake, shake our feet
> We're gonna shake, shake, shake, shake, shake our feet

Encore!

Other body parts you can shake are:

• toes	• elbows	• head	• tummy
• fingers	• knees	• whole body	
• arms	• legs		

Spotlight on . . .
PHYSICAL & MOTOR
DEVELOPMENT

Director's note

This is a great way to get out the wiggles.

Act it out!

1. Count "1, 2, 3, 4, 5, 6, 7, 8" while shaking your left hand. Vigorously shake your hand for each number.

2. Shake your right hand counting up to eight, then your left foot counting to eight, then your right foot again eight times.

3. Next, count "1, 2, 3, 4, 5, 6" while shaking your left hand, then "1, 2, 3, 4, 5, 6" while shaking your right hand, then "1, 2, 3, 4, 5, 6" while shaking your left foot, then "1, 2, 3, 4, 5, 6" while shaking your right foot.

4. Continue this pattern of shaking your hands and feet while counting "1, 2, 3, 4" and "1, 2."

5. On 1, shake everything all over.

Director's note

This is another high-energy shakedown to get the wiggles out.

Spotlight on . . .
PHYSICAL & MOTOR
DEVELOPMENT

Circle Dance

Act it out!

1. Do the circle dance! Have children stand in a circle. Make sure children are spread out so they have plenty of space to work. Consider doing the "Circle Stretch" (page 40) before you start. Instruct actors to make circles with their:

   - left arm, right arm, both arms
   - left wrist, right wrist, both wrists
   - left leg, right leg
   - left ankle, right ankle
   - head, neck
   - mouth
   - shoulders
   - stomach
   - knees

2. Finish the circle dance by inviting the students to make as many circles with different body parts as they can, at once.

Encore!

Instruct children to make a certain number of circles with a specific body part, such as:

   - five circles with their arms
   - four circles with their wrists
   - one circle with their knee

Spotlight on . . .
PHYSICAL & MOTOR
DEVELOPMENT

Act it out!

1. Have all the children find a spot on the floor.

2. The teacher will lead the class through this imaginative journey. Tell the group that today you are going to make popcorn. All of the children are popcorn kernels. Can they roll up into kernels, squatting on the floor?

3. Guide the actors through the activity. "As the pan gets hotter, the kernels will begin to pop, becoming popcorn. When you pop, you jump in the air, clapping your hands over your head. The popping should be gradual but build up toward the end. So at first, there will be a few popcorn kernels popping, but by the end everyone will be popping. You may pop more than once. Are you ready? I am putting the popcorn pan on the stove."

4. Inform the class that you are removing the pan from the stovetop to stop the popcorn from popping and prevent it from burning. When the pan is off the stovetop, the popcorn kernels must stop popping.

Head, Shoulders, Knees, and Toes
· ·

Act it out!

1. Sing the childhood favorite, "Head, Shoulders, Knees, and Toes" along with the actions to warm up the voice and body.

> Head and shoulders knees and toes
> Knees and toes
> Head and shoulders knees and toes
> Knees and toes
> And eyes and ears
> And mouth and nose
> Head and shoulders knees and toes
> Knees and toes

2. After the actors are comfortable and know the words and actions, explore performing the song slower, faster, or extra fast.

Act it out!

1. Invite participants to stand in a circle and do the "Hokey Pokey." Make sure everyone performs the accompanying actions:

> You put your right hand in,
> You put your right hand out,
> You put your right hand in,
> And you shake it all about.
> You do the Hokey Pokey
> And you turn yourself around,
> That's what it's all about.

Complete the song with these other verses, if you wish:

- left hand
- right foot
- left foot
- head
- rear
- whole self

CHAPTER SIX

....

Imaginative Play

Drama is an important tool for developing imagination. In some drama games, children must imagine different environments and what it's like to be in these different spaces. They become different animals and characters. Experiencing a character's perspective promotes empathy as well as tolerance and understanding. Make-believe games also promote the development of self-regulation, such as reduced aggression, civility, and the delay of gratification (Kaufman, Singer, and Singer 2012).

Cultivating imagination also promotes creative thinking and problem solving. Early pretend play can enhance young children's capacity for cognitive flexibility and creativity. During many imaginative dramatic activities, children must problem solve together and communicate their ideas and needs to others in the group. Taking on different roles also provides young children with the chance to develop important social skills, such as communication and problem solving. Imaginative play is vital to all early childhood spaces, but especially during drama class. Research has shown that an early childhood curriculum that contains elements of pretend play leads to more curious and imaginative students, engendering an engagement to learning and lifelong creative thinkers (Kaufman, Singer, and Singer 2012).

Pass the Beanbag

Materials

o beanbags

Act it out!

1. Pair each child with a partner.

2. Give each pair one beanbag.

3. Have the partners practice passing the beanbag to each other, imagining the beanbag as different things. The beanbag could be:

   • a birthday present   • a prickly porcupine

   • a heavy bowling ball   • a soft, cuddly kitten

   • an injured baby bird   • a cactus

   • a water balloon

Wake the Dragons!

Materials

o medieval music (optional)

Act it out!

1. Instruct students to lie down on the floor on their backs with their eyes open. Begin playing medieval music for this activity.

2. One student will be the dragon that is awake. The awake dragon will try to make other dragons wake up by making these dragons smile or laugh.

3. If the awake dragon succeeds in making another dragon smile or laugh, then that dragon will wake up and try to make other sleeping dragons smile or laugh.

4. Play until every dragon is awake.

5. If the group wants to play the game again and time allows, let a willing volunteer or the person who was the last dragon to wake up be the first dragon in the new game.

Director's note

Remind participants not to walk or jump over other dragons, touch other dragons, or get too close to sleeping dragons. Remind them that in drama class, we are respectful and take care of each other so that everyone has fun!

Materials

○ a bag or pillowcase full of puppets, props, or stuffed animals

Act it out!

1. Have children sit in a circle.

2. Say, "Once upon a time," and pull out an item from the story bag. Come up with a few lines of a story using that item.

3. Pass the bag to the next child in the circle. Allow the child to pull out an item and add a few lines to the story you started.

4. Play until the entire class has had an opportunity to pull out an item and add to the story. Finish the story when it comes back to you. Then say, "And they all lived happily ever after. The end!"

Spotlight on . . .
SOCIAL & EMOTIONAL
LEARNING

CREATIVITY &
THE ARTS

Lily Pad Hop!

Materials

○ fun music

○ Hula-Hoops

Act it out!

1. Ask the children, "What would it be like to spend a day in the life of a frog? What would frogs like to do? What would frogs be afraid of? What would frogs see?"

2. Lay Hula-Hoops on the floor around the classroom.

3. Tell participants that they are frogs on a pond covered with lily pads. You may need to explain or show them a picture or painting of a pond with lily pads, such as the work of French impressionist Claude Monet. Children can hop from lily pad to lily pad as they wish. They can pretend to swim through the water when they are not seated on a lily pad. They can try to catch flies with their tongues. They can ribbit to communicate with each other.

4. At the end of the activity, invite the children to share what they are doing as frogs.

Encore!

Read a book about frogs on a pond, such as *It's Mine!* by Leo Lionni, or look at a picture or painting of a pond to help the children understand more about the habitat and what it's like being a frog on a pond.

Spotlight on . . .
CREATIVITY &
THE ARTS

PHYSICAL & MOTOR
DEVELOPMENT

Act it out!

1. To take your students on an imaginary boat trip, have actors sit in two lines, facing you. Make sure everyone can see you.

2. Tell them they are all on a rowboat together. The sea is calm, but the waves rock the boat a little (sway your body). What does the ocean breeze sound like? (Perhaps it sounds like blowing air through your teeth, or perhaps actors will come up with another way to make the ocean breeze.) Let's use our oars to row the boat (pantomime rowing a boat). Look at the seagulls! What do they sound like? (Allow the children to make gull noises.) What do we see in the distance? (Hold up your hand as though looking in the distance.) Let's get out our telescopes (pantomime looking through a telescope). What can we see? (Have them tell you; add these ideas and observations to the story.) All right, let's start fishing! Let's throw our fishing rods into the ocean (pantomime casting a line into the sea). Has anyone caught anything? (Let them tell you. Let the fish go or catch something, like a pop bottle, that needs to be recycled. Save it to recycle later so you can keep the ocean clean and protect the wildlife.) Oh, no! Look at those storm clouds overhead (point to storm clouds). Listen, the wind is picking up. Can you hear it? (Make the sound of the wind blowing.) It's raining (snap fingers). Harder! (Drum your hands on the floor.) Harder! (Stomp your feet on the floor.) Let's row toward shore! (Row.) Which way was the shore? My compass isn't working! (Let students point to shore.)

3. Let the actors decide the ending for this activity. Perhaps the class will row to safety and get out on shore, or maybe the boat overturns and the class has to swim to shore.

Spotlight on . . .
CREATIVITY &
THE ARTS

SOCIAL & EMOTIONAL
LEARNING

Pet Show!

Act it out!

1. Divide students into pairs. One child will be the pet owner and the other child will be the pet.

2. Give each pair a couple of minutes to think of a pet, the pet's name, and a trick the pet can perform. They can have any kind of pet (even a *T. rex* doing ballet).

3. Put on a pet show in which the pet owner tells everyone what type of pet she has and what the pet's name is. Then the pet does a trick.

4. Give every pet and owner a round of applause after their trick.

5. Students switch roles for the next round and have another pet show.

Spotlight on . . .
CREATIVITY &
THE ARTS

SOCIAL & EMOTIONAL
LEARNING

Act it out!

1. Instruct children to sit in a circle.

2. Pull an imaginary box out of your pocket.

3. Show the children how you can make the box bigger or smaller, lighter or heavier, using your hands.

4. Pull an imaginary item out of the box and perform an action using that object. For example, if it's a toothbrush, pretend to brush your teeth. Have students try to guess what the object is.

5. After they have guessed, pass the box on to the next child.

6. Ask the child to show the rest of the group how big or small and light or heavy the box is. Ask him to show the class how to use the object he pulled out of the box.

7. Play until everyone has had an opportunity to pull something out of the box.

Spotlight on . . .
COGNITIVE
DEVELOPMENT

CREATIVITY &
THE ARTS

Artists and Statues

Materials

o music

Act it out!

1. Divide children into pairs. One student will be the artist and the other will be the statue.

2. Allow the artist to tell the other child to move their body into a statue.

3. Play music while the artists are working and stop it when it is time to stop sculpting.

4. Have all the artists walk around and look at the statues as though they are visiting a museum. The children who are statues should remain frozen so the visitors at the museum can see what the artists created. Encourage students to come up with titles for their masterpieces or talk briefly about their statues.

5. Switch roles and let the statues be the artists and the artists be the statues.

Encore!

This is a great activity when learning about art, such as Edgar Degas's sculpture *The Little Dancer*. Then pair it with the book *Degas and the Little Dancer* by Laurence Anholt.

Spotlight on . . .
PHYSICAL & MOTOR
DEVELOPMENT

CREATIVITY &
THE ARTS

Act it out!

1. Participants stand in a circle. Explain what doing something "in place" means. Model running, jumping, and dancing in place so the children understand the concept.

2. One at a time, give each student an opportunity to think of a sport for the class to pantomime.

3. Each student will say, "We're playing," followed by a sport. Then, while standing in place, actors will pretend to play that sport with each other, using their imaginations. Regroup before moving on to the next child.

Encore!

Here are some different sports students can play:

- American football
- jumping rope
- rowing
- snowboarding
- soccer

- surfing
- swimming
- tennis
- volleyball

You can also play this game by pantomiming the playing of different musical instruments. Here are some examples:

- cymbals
- drums
- flute
- guitar
- harmonica

- harp
- piano
- trumpet
- violin

Or pantomime eating different foods:

- apple
- banana
- chocolate milk with a straw
- spicy hot sauce (you all might need a drink of water)

- hot soup
- ice cream
- extra-sticky peanut butter
- spaghetti

Spotlight on . . .
CREATIVITY &
THE ARTS

PHYSICAL & MOTOR
DEVELOPMENT

Materials

○ various costume pieces

Act it out!

1. Display various costume pieces. Allow participants to create a character using the different costume pieces. Give them five to ten minutes to create a character. If children struggle with sharing, hand out one costume piece or prop to each child and invite them to create a character based on the item they were given. Or the children can take turns picking out costume pieces. Children can also create their character at home and bring their costume pieces to school, taking them out and putting them on during drama class. Do what is the best fit for your community.

2. Have a party (such as a fancy dress party, tea party, or another party the children choose) and let the different characters mingle with each other. This activity can be loosely structured or, as a teacher-in-role, you can narrate the story of what is happening at the party. Think carefully about what your role will be in the activity. Perhaps you are the hostess or host of the party. Children can also sit in pairs and chat together as their different characters.

Spotlight on . . .
CREATIVITY &
THE ARTS

SOCIAL & EMOTIONAL
LEARNING

A Sandwich

Act it out!

1. Build an imaginary sandwich as a class.

2. Have each person add something to the sandwich. As the teacher, announce each child's addition to the sandwich so the group knows what kind of sandwich you now have, such as a "peanut butter, cheese, ketchup, bubble gum sandwich."

3. When the sandwich is complete, pantomime taking a huge bite as a class. Have the children describe what the sandwich is like. Is the sandwich chewy from the bubble gum? Sticky from the peanut butter? Crunchy from the chips? Soggy from the ketchup? Does it stay together or fall apart? Do they like how it tastes or not? Make sure to pantomime the entire process very clearly for the children.

Spotlight on . . .
CREATIVITY &
THE ARTS

Encore!

You can also do this with an ice cream sundae or a fruit or vegetable salad.

Materials

o picnic basket (optional)

o picnic blanket (optional)

o a calming woodland soundscape (optional)

Act it out!

1. Have the children sit in a circle on the picnic blanket and put the basket in the center of the group. If you do not have a blanket or basket, just pantomime having one.

2. Tell them you are going on a picnic and everyone brought something to share with the group.

3. Model for students how to pantomime taking things from the basket and eating the food.

4. Pass the basket around and let everyone pantomime taking some food item from the basket.

5. Each child pantomimes giving everyone in the group the food she brought. Everyone then pretends to eat the food. If they don't like the food, then they can abstain by saying, "No, thank you."

Encore!

You can also have the children pantomime packing the basket with their items. You can then walk around the space to find a good picnic spot and unpack the picnic. Again, this is something you can adjust to fit your classroom.

Spotlight on . . .
CREATIVITY &
THE ARTS

PHYSICAL & MOTOR
DEVELOPMENT

Friendship Soup

Materials

o large cooking pot (optional)

Act it out!

1. Create a pot of friendship soup. Have participants sit in a circle around a large cooking pot, real or imagined.

2. Tell them, "We are going to make vegetable soup using our imaginations."

3. Ask everyone, "What kind of vegetables go into soup?"

4. Ask every child to provide a vegetable for the soup that they pass out to the rest of the class or to you.

5. Allow the students to pantomime washing, peeling, and chopping different imaginary vegetables.

6. Put their imaginary vegetables into the pot. Ask them to add more logs to the fire for boiling the soup.

7. The children stir the soup with their imaginary spoons. Invite them to try the soup, blowing on their imaginary spoons to make sure it isn't too hot.

8. Add imaginary salt and pepper as necessary. Perhaps the pepper makes everyone sneeze. Taste the soup a few times to make sure you have the right amount. Add it slowly so you don't add too much.

9. Dish out the soup in imaginary bowls and eat it together. Blow on the bowls if it's too hot to eat right away.

Spotlight on . . .
CREATIVITY &
THE ARTS

SOCIAL & EMOTIONAL
LEARNING

Follow the Flock

Act it out!

1. Discuss why and how birds migrate. By flying in a V formation, birds carefully position their wingtips and synchronize their flapping to catch the preceding bird's updraft—and save energy during their long flight.

2. As the teacher, you will be the leader, leading the flock. The children, or other birds, will get behind you in a V shape. Like follow the leader, the other birds will try to follow your movements exactly as you move around the space.

3. Create a story, as a class, of the adventure you go on as a flock of birds.

4. Ask your class various questions about what is happening during your migration so you are creating the story together. "What might our flock see flying through the air? What will we fly over during our adventure? What will the weather be like? Will the air be warm or cold? How do we feel right now? Are we excited, scared, or tired?" Think about all these elements as you fly your flock through the sky.

Spotlight on . . .
SOCIAL & EMOTIONAL
LEARNING

PHYSICAL & MOTOR
DEVELOPMENT

Encore!

This is an excellent game to play during the fall, when discussing how seasons change or how some animals migrate.

Spotlight on . . .
SOCIAL & EMOTIONAL
LEARNING

Materials

o various costumes

o certificates for each student

Act it out!

This is a great end-of-the-year activity.

1. Host an award ceremony for the class.

2. Create a certificate for each student that highlights his strengths.

3. Allow the children to dress up in finery. They can even walk down a red carpet where they are photographed and briefly interviewed.

4. Be a flamboyant host, and present everyone with an award. Let the students make brief thank-you speeches if they want.

Pass the Prop . . .

Materials

o a bag full of fun props

Act it out!

1. Have students stand in a circle.

2. One at a time, invite each child to pull a silly prop from the bag.

3. Challenge each child to use the prop in a different way than it was intended. Encourage the students to share with the group what the prop is. For example, one child could pull out a handkerchief and say it is a cape. The next child might pull out the same handkerchief and say it is a mustache.

4. Pass the bag around the circle. Play until everyone who wants a turn has had a turn or until students are emotionally ready to move on. Allow students to say "pass" if they wish or ask for help from their peers to come up with what the prop might be.

Spotlight on . . .
CREATIVITY &
THE ARTS

Encore!

You can also play this game by passing the same prop around and seeing if everyone can come up with a different idea of what the same prop is. For example, you could pass a jump rope around. One person might say it is a snake, another a necklace, a third a huge piece of spaghetti, etc.

Materials

o a backpack or knapsack (optional)

Act it out!

1. Tell the children, "We are going on an adventure and we need to pack."

2. Each child will pantomime packing something she thinks the class might need for the adventure. You should go first to model how to do this.

3. Take the time to use each item before you pack it. For example, if you pack water, pantomime twisting the cap off and taking a drink. Or, if it's sunblock, pantomime rubbing it on your face and arms. If it's a warm hat, scarf, and mittens, pantomime passing the items out to everyone and putting them on. If it's tennis shoes, pantomime putting them on and tying the laces.

4. Let each child come up with something to pack, with everyone pantomiming using the object.

Encore!

Children can pack for various kinds of adventures, such as:

o a day at the beach

o school

o the jungle

o the North Pole

o the desert

o up a high mountain

o at the park

Spotlight on . . .
CREATIVITY &
THE ARTS

COGNITIVE
DEVELOPMENT

Act it out!

1. Have the children sit in a circle.

2. Tell the students a story about a day at the beach. Allow them to create sound effects and pantomime various parts of the story. Here are some examples of events you can include:

   - We woke up in the morning (yawn, roll over, go back to sleep, get shaken awake, yawn again), stretched (stretch), got dressed (ask everyone what you should wear to the beach; pantomime putting on those items), brushed our teeth (pantomime brushing teeth) and hair (pantomime brushing hair), and ate breakfast (ask them what they are eating for breakfast; pantomime eating that item, whether it's a bowl of cereal, pancakes, or a smoothie).

   - Ask the class, "What do we pack?" (Pantomime packing the various items you need for a day at the beach.)

   - We rode bikes (have children lie on their backs to pretend to ride bikes and move legs like on a bike), or rode in the car (pretend they are driving a car).

   - We rubbed on plenty of sunblock (pretend to rub sunblock all over your body and ask children why we put on sunblock—make sure to get your nose and behind the ears).

   - We dug a moat on the shoreline using our hands or a toy shovel (pantomime digging a moat with your hands or a toy shovel). Ask the children to describe how the sand feels. Maybe the moat collapses and you have to start all over again. When you finish, maybe everyone dances and stomps the castle into the ground. Maybe you find a shell or crab while you are digging.

   - We swam in the water (swim around the classroom; have everyone lie down to back float on a raft for a while).

   - We dried off with our towels, then laid them back down to dry. (Pretend to dry yourself off with a towel. Brush sand off your feet first. Make sure to dry off your hair. Name the different body parts as you dry them. Lay the towels out and let everyone lie on a towel and sunbathe.) Ask the children to describe what sounds they hear. The waves? Seagulls? Children laughing and splashing in the water? Someone selling ice cream?

   - We built a sand castle. (Pretend to build a sand castle. Ask the children to describe how the sand feels. What does the sand castle look like?)

- We got kind of hot, so we drank some lemonade. (Pretend to drink lemonade. Wipe your mouth off with your arm, or slurp the beverage up with a straw.)

- We swam in the water again (pantomime swimming).

- We saw fish (make a fish face with your lips, and use your hands as gills).

- We lay on the beach to dry off (lie on your towel and sunbathe).

- We heard seagulls (make seagull noises).

- We saw seagulls flying overhead (make seagulls with your hands).

- We ate some ice cream. (Pretend to eat ice cream. Ask the children what flavor they have. Eat the ice cream quickly so it doesn't melt down your hand.)

- We saw a crab scuttling along the shore (make a crab with your hands, and scuttle your crab along the floor).

- We played with our beach ball (pretend to throw a ball).

- We ate a picnic lunch. What was in our picnic lunch? (Pretend to eat those foods.)

3. You can ask children what else might happen on a day at the beach and let them participate in the telling of the story. There are many ways to end the story. You can end the story with ideas like these:

- We drove or rode our bikes home (pretend to drive a car or lie on your backs and pretend to ride bikes).

- We took a shower (pretend to take a shower; make sure to cover yourself with soap and shampoo your hair really well).

- We brushed our teeth (pretend to brush your teeth, and floss too).

- We put on our pajamas (act out getting dressed in pajamas).

- We went to bed, pulled up the covers, and fell fast asleep (pantomime getting tucked into bed and falling asleep).

Encore!

You can also take children on various other excursions, such as:

- a day at the zoo

- a day at the art museum

- a visit to the grocery store

- a day at school

- a rainy day

- a snowy day

- a day camping

- a visit to a pond

- a picnic

Spotlight on . . .
CREATIVITY &
THE ARTS

APPROACHES TO
LEARNING

Magic Carpet Ride

Materials

o a carpet (optional) or a carpet drawn in chalk outside

Act it out!

1. Have the children sit on a carpet.

2. Tell them the carpet is magic. They will ride it high in the sky.

3. Ask them what they see below. What is the weather like in the sky?

4. Have the class imagine that the carpet is landing in different locations, and let the children get off and explore places like these:

   • a park   • a jungle

   • a forest   • the ocean

   • a playground   • the North Pole

   • a mountaintop   • an apple orchard

1. Let the children come up with some of the locations.

2. When it's time to leave, tell children it's time to get back onto the carpet. If they are hesitant, come up with some emergency that fits the location they are currently visiting. For example, if the class is in the prehistoric ages, tell the children a *T. rex* is coming and they had better hurry back to the carpet.

3. Bring the game to a close by landing the carpet safely in the classroom. Ask the children to vacate the carpet and say good-bye to it. Roll the carpet up and put it away for another day.

Spotlight on . . .
CREATIVITY &
THE ARTS

COGNITIVE
DEVELOPMENT

Magic Train Ride

Materials

o masking tape (optional)

o chalk (optional)

Act it out!

1. Create train tracks using masking tape on the floor or draw tracks with chalk outside (although tracks aren't necessary).

2. Instruct the children to get in a line, putting their hands on the shoulders of the person in front of them.

3. The students travel along the tracks or around the space as a train.

4. Have the train stop at different destinations and let the children explore these environments, similar to how you explored different places in the game "Magic Carpet Ride" (page 74). The train can stop in various locations, such as:

- the beach
- a winter wonderland
- an amusement park
- prehistoric times

- a desert
- the grocery store
- school

5. Call, "All aboard" when it is time for the students to get back on the train (get back in line).

Dancing Feet

Materials

o magic wand

o wizard hat (optional)

Act it out!

1. Tell the class you are a wizard. You will wave your wand to cast a spell that gives the children different kinds of feet.

2. Allow the kids to walk freely around the space. Use huge gestures and say silly magic words before telling the kids what kind of feet they have next.

3. Let them move around the space freely, using types of feet like these:

- dancing feet
- skipping feet
- hopping feet
- marching feet
- sliding feet
- slow feet
- tiny-steps feet
- long-steps feet
- ballerina feet
- bunny rabbit feet
- frozen feet

Materials

- different colors of masking tape
- pictures that reflect the day's theme

Act it out!

1. Create four different dance moves themed around what the children are learning about in class. For example, if they are learning about animals in the ocean, invent a crab dance, a fish dance, a shark dance, and an octopus dance.

2. Divide the classroom into four different quadrants using masking tape. Designate each area for a specific type of dance, such as one area for the crab dance, another for the fish dance. Place pictures of the animals near the four quadrants. Practice dancing as the different animals as a class before you start.

3. Allow the class to dance wherever they wish, but their dance must match whichever designated area they are standing in. Participate with them so they understand the game and to enhance the fun for all involved.

Spotlight on . . .
PHYSICAL & MOTOR
DEVELOPMENT

Pass the Face

Act it out!

1. Have the children sit or stand in a group.

2. Have one child begin by making a facial expression to the child next to him.

3. The child next to him will try to replicate that facial expression and pass it to the child next to her.

4. Pass the facial expression all the way around the circle.

5. Play until everyone has gotten the chance to be the first to start a facial expression.

Spotlight on . . .
SOCIAL & EMOTIONAL
LEARNING

Materials

o a large mirror (optional)

Act it out!

1. Have the children sit in front of a large mirror. They can also sit in a circle facing each other if you do not have a large mirror.

2. Instruct all the students to cover their faces.

3. Tell them that when you say, "peekaboo" they should move their hands away from their face and make a face depicting a specific emotion into the mirror. Demonstrate for them. Say, "Happy face" and "peekaboo" (move hands and reveal a happy face). Cover your face. Say, "Sad face" and "peekaboo" (move hands and show a sad face). Faces they can make include the following:

  • sad face

  • happy face

  • silly face

  • angry face

  • scared face

  • surprised face

  • sleepy face

  • scrunched-up-tight face

  • wide-open face

Spotlight on . . .
SOCIAL & EMOTIONAL
LEARNING

Today I . . .

Act it out!

1. One at a time, have the children share one thing they did during the day. First, demonstrate for them one thing that you did that day.

2. The rest of the class will then act out doing that thing.

3. You can have the children do this activity in a circle, in place, or moving freely around the classroom.

Encore!

  Ideas to encourage students who are stuck include the following:

  • brushed my teeth

  • took a nap

  • played with toys

  • drew a picture

  • drank milk

Spotlight on . . .
PHYSICAL & MOTOR
DEVELOPMENT

Familiar Favorites

Charades

....

Materials

o charade cards with pictures

Act it out!

1. Have the class stand in a circle. You can also let the children work in small groups or pairs.

2. Let a child pick a card, then have her act out for the rest of the group what is on the card. The rest of the class must guess what she is acting out.

Encore!

For younger children, make the clues they are to act out very easy: reading a book, sleeping, happy, sad, dog, cat. Use picture cards instead of written words (you can even cut pictures out of a magazine). If you use cards with words, you may need to whisper in the child's ear what the card says.

If a child is nervous working by herself, let a friend act with her or allow her to just observe and participate when and if she feels ready.

Spotlight on . . .
SOCIAL & EMOTIONAL
LEARNING

CHAPTER SEVEN

···

Creative Movement

Creative movement helps energize the body for creative play. These activities are also a good source of exercise and promote healthy living. Creative movement activities develop bodily intelligence, also known as kinesthetic intelligence—the ability to control one's bodily motions and handle objects skillfully for expressive as well as goal-directed purposes—and fine- and gross-motor skills (Gardner 1983). In his 1983 book, *Frames of Mind*, Howard Gardner describes how nurturing bodily intelligence is a vital part of any classroom curriculum. Learning is enhanced for many students when their bodies are involved. For primarily bodily learners, engaging them through expressive creative movement enhances their learning of various topics and is a primary way that they communicate and express themselves. These types of theatre games allow students to explore with their bodies while developing imagination, coordination, and bodily awareness.

Safety and structure is vital during a creative movement session. Remind students to be aware of where their bodies are in relation to other students and objects in the classroom. Always remind students to be aware of and respect their bodies, as well as their peers' bodies. You may need to remind some students not to touch their peers' bodies during some games.

If you feel that participants aren't in control of their bodies or are making choices that aren't safe, pause the activity temporarily by playing the game "If You Are Listening" (page 19), or use another classroom-focusing tool to get students refocused and centered so you can safely proceed with the drama activity. You can say, "I appreciate how all of you are participating and so energetic, but we need to be safe with our bodies so no one gets hurt. Be in control of your body and aware of where everyone else is around you."

Music can help create the emotional climate of the drama class and can guide students in making expressive movement choices during a creative movement activity. Start and stop music to communicate to participants when an activity is starting and ending. You can also stop the music if you feel students need a moment to re-center or take a break during the creative movement activity.

Use guided discovery during a creative movement activity. Ask students questions and let them make discoveries and reach solutions through expressive movement (Kaufmann 2005, 33). Use colorful words for your movement prompts that ignite the imaginations of small children. Descriptive words such as *travel*, *float*, *wiggle*, *gallop*, *hop*, *shake*, *quick*, *light*, *high*, and *low* all ignite the imaginations of small children as they explore using their bodies, space, energy, time, and relationships to one another and their environment (Kaufmann 2005). Here is a list of descriptive movement words you can use to inspire and ignite the imaginations of your students.

Descriptive Movement Words to Guide Creative Movement Activities

Speed of Movement

fast/slow	hurried	quick	start/stop

Qualities of Movement

agile	gentle	loose	soft
brisk	graceful	nimble	sudden
calm	hard	relaxed	
careful	heavy	serene	
fast/quick	light	smooth	

Movement Through Space

above/below	behind/in front of	diagonal	sideways
across	below	high/low	through
apart	beside	inside/outside	up/down
away/toward	between	left/right	zigzag
backward/forward	cross	on/off	

Types of Movement: Locomotor (from one place to another)

climb	glide	shuffle	swing
crab walk	grow	skip	tiptoe
crawl	hop	sleep	travel
creep	jump	slide	waddle
dance	leap	slither	walk
drive	meander	soar	waltz
drop	nap	spring	wiggle
flap	prance	stomp	wobble
fly	roll	stroll	
gallop	scamper	swim	

balance	curl/straighten	shake	turn
bend	dig	shrug	twirl
blink	duck	sit/stand	twist
bow/curtsy	extend	slide	wave
catch/throw	freeze	snap	wink
chew	grab/release	stretch	wipe
circular	lie down	sway	yawn
clap	rise/fall	swing	
close/open	rock	tap	

Move Like a . . .

Type of animal	Type of person
bear	basketball player dribbling the ball down the court
cat	firefighter putting out a fire
dog	king or queen waving to a crowd
elephant	mountain climber scaling a mountain
monkey	scuba diver swimming in the ocean surrounded by a
mouse	colorful school of fish
songbird	
tiger	

Add pantomiming an activity or environment to further ignite the children's imaginations, or ask the class for an activity or environment for the character or animal.

Move in an . . .

Activity	Environment
cooking	crawling through the hot desert
dancing	ice skating on a pond during a snowstorm
gardening	swimming in the ocean
painting	walking through the thick underbrush of the jungle
shopping	

Expressive Adverbs

angrily	happily	sadly	tearfully
excitedly	hurriedly	sleepily	
fearfully	joyfully	sneakily	

Parts of the Body

arms	feet	legs	spine
back	fingers	lungs	stomach
chest	hands	mouth	toes
chin	heart	neck	wrists
elbows	hips	nose	
eyes	knees	shoulders	

The more specific you are with language, the more specific the children's movements will be. In Patricia Reedy's 2003 book, *Body, Mind, & Spirit in Action*, the author describes the importance of using imaginative and well-worded prompts during a creative movement or dance session: "This facilitates the learning process, as the child connects linguistic, kinesthetic, spatial, temporal, and energetic concepts in action and idea" (17). For example, use colorful descriptions such as, "tiptoe like a frightened mouse trying not to wake up the sleeping cat," instead of just "tiptoe." Encourage children to explore with moving high and low in space, as well as moving at different speeds and using different body parts. Stillness and silence are also important as these moments can encourage impulse control and self-soothing, as well as help children become aware of their body's boundaries (Hirsh 2004).

Young children love moving and creative play. Aim to include a creative movement activity in every drama class. Feel free to incorporate music, literature, props, costumes, music, and puppetry, depending on what topic the class is learning about that day. These tools will contribute to a fun and creative environment and classroom culture.

Jump and Jive!
Creative Movement Activities

Grumpy Bear

Materials

○ fun, upbeat music or a woodland soundscape

Act it out!

1. Children are all woodland creatures dancing in the forest. Let them choose what woodland creature they would like to be, such as a bunny, bird, butterfly, frog, or others.

2. Play the music and allow children to move around freely as woodland creatures.

3. Freeze the music, and call out, "Grumpy bear!" Pretend to be a grumpy bear, rumbling through the forest.

4. All the woodland creatures have to freeze! Let them know when the grumpy bear is gone, so they can move again. Playing the music is one way to let them know it is now safe to move.

5. At the end of class, while the actors are still frozen, tap the students one at a time on the shoulder, or gather in a circle and have them share with everyone what animal they were.

Encore!

You can also discuss what kind of animals students could be, or read a book that takes place in a forest, such as these:

• *Because of an Acorn* by Lola M. Schaefer

• *The Busy Tree* by Jennifer Ward

• *Lost in the Woods* by Carl R. Sams

• *I Am a Bunny* by Ole Risom

Or look at famous artwork depicting woodland creatures, such as these:

• *Red Deer II* by Franz Marc

• *Young Hare* by Albrecht Dürer

Or you could try this idea for something more fantastical:

• *Raven Addressing the Assembled Animals* by Miskin

This is a great activity for balance and coordination.

Spotlight on . . .
PHYSICAL & MOTOR
DEVELOPMENT

Look What My Hands Can Do!

Act it out!

1. Have children stand in a circle. Say, "Look what my hands can do. They can turn book pages." Pantomime turning book pages.

2. Say, "Let's all turn book pages." Everyone in the circle can then pantomime turning book pages.

3. Go around the circle, having each child come up with something that their hands can do. Each student should begin by saying, "Look what my hands can do. They can . . ." Here is a list of different things that hands can do:

• play piano

• tie shoes

• clap

• snap

• hold a sandwich

• brush teeth

• color in a book

• fingerpaint

• hold a ball

• play a drum

• give high fives

• open a gift

Spotlight on . . .
PHYSICAL & MOTOR
DEVELOPMENT

Materials

o a large, wacky hat

o cards with various action words and animal pictures

Act it out!

1. Have participants stand in a circle. Remind children what it means to do an action "in place." Demonstrate for them running or performing another activity in place. Also establish a sound or an action that means it's time to freeze, such as blowing on a kazoo, touching the floor, saying a silly word like "bum-fuzzle," "taradiddle," or "cattywampus," or bringing out a puppet that says, "Everybody freeze!" very obnoxiously. Let the actors practice running in place and freezing when you give the signal. It's important for everyone to freeze when directed during this activity so the class can move on together and hear the next directions.

2. Pass the hat to the first child.

3. The child will pull a card from the hat and share with the class what the animal in the picture is. The child will then hand you the card. You will have to read the text or explain the action the students will act out. The child should set down the hat. Put the card in your pocket or set it aside so there are only new cards in the hat.

4. The entire class will then perform, as a group, whatever action the participant pulled out of the hat.

5. After they have completed acting out the card, signal them to freeze so you can move on to the next card. The first student will pass the hat to the next child, who will pull out a card and continue the activity.

6. It's preferable to play until everyone has gotten a turn. Allow students to say, "No, thank you" if they are too nervous to pull out a card and share it with the class.

Encore!

Here is a list of some actions you can put on cards:

- hop like a frog
- hop like a bunny
- do the chicken dance
- stomp and roar like a *T. rex*
- trumpet like an elephant

- fly like a butterfly
- twirl like a ballerina
- yawn
- give your neighbors a high five
- mix a bowl of cookie dough

This game also makes a great warm-up.

Spotlight on . . .
PHYSICAL & MOTOR
DEVELOPMENT

Materials

o dice

Act it out!

1. Have the children stand in a circle facing each other.

2. One participant at a time will throw a die.

3. Together, the children have to jump like frogs as many times as the die says. Count aloud.

4. Let everyone have an opportunity to throw the die.

5. If you want to go around again, have the actors jump like a different animal, such as these:

   • kangaroo

   • bunny

Encore!

You can also let the children choose what animal they will jump as or what movement they will perform each time. For example, an actor could choose jumping jacks, hopping on one foot, clapping their hands or stomping their feet. The class would then do that action the number of times the die roll says. This is a great activity for practicing counting.

Spotlight on . . .
PHYSICAL & MOTOR
DEVELOPMENT

Yes, Let's . . .

Act it out!

1. Have the group stand in a circle.

2. You will begin by saying, "Let's run in place."

3. Everyone else will reply, "Yes, let's run in place," and then run in place.

4. Go around the circle and give each actor the opportunity to say, "Let's . . ." and let everyone come up with an idea to share with the group.

Director's note

You may need to remind the actors what it means to do something "in place" before you start. Prepare in advance a word or signal that means "freeze" or "stop."

Spotlight on . . .
PHYSICAL & MOTOR
DEVELOPMENT

Materials

o a playlist of various sounds, such as:

• a car beeping

• a lion roaring

• an elephant trumpeting

• a duck quacking

• a police car siren

• a dog barking

• a baby crying

• someone snoring

• a cat meowing

Act it out!

1. Allow the children to walk around the space freely but silently.

2. Explain that when you play a sound, they have to silently act out, in place, what they think is making the sound. Tell the actors to freeze in place when you turn off the sound.

3. Play a sound from the playlist.

4. Have the children silently act out what they think the sound is.

5. Turn off the sound and remind them to freeze in place.

6. You will touch someone and that person will share with the class what he is.

7. Touch a few people. Or you can ask the whole class what they thought the sound was.

8. When you start the new sound, the children can move again. Allow the children to move around as though they are the new object, person, or animal making that sound.

Spotlight on . . .
PHYSICAL & MOTOR
DEVELOPMENT

Act it out!

1. Divide the students into three groups with an equal number of children and give each group a number, one, two, or three.

2. With the class standing in a circle, you will call out a number and an action.

3. If you call out, "One and snakes," all the actors in group one will slither across the circle and take the spot of one of their classmates in the circle. Do the same for the groups two and three, using a new action each time.

Director's note

The concept of taking the spot of another student in the circle can be challenging for some classes. You can mark the spots in the circle with stickers or masking tape so children can clearly see the empty spots in the circle. You can also have students line up at one end of the classroom and cross the classroom with your specific instruction when you call out their numbers. This can be less confusing to some children.

Encore!

Cater the different ways to cross the circle to the themes for the day. For example, if you are learning about the rain forest, you can have a group cross as:

- ants
- butterflies
- jaguars
- monkeys
- parrots
- sloths
- snakes
- toucans
- tree frogs

Spotlight on . . .
PHYSICAL & MOTOR
DEVELOPMENT

Find the Cow, Chicken, Pig

Act it out!

1. Have all the children lie down on the floor with their eyes closed.

2. Go around and whisper either "cow," "chicken," or "pig" in each child's ear.

3. When everyone has a designated animal, instruct all the animals to wake up. Without words, the students need to find the other members of their group using only their actions.

Encore!

You can also whisper two to four other animals, depending on what your theme is. For example, if you're learning about metamorphosis, you could whisper either "butterfly" or "caterpillar."

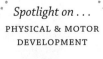

Spotlight on . . .
PHYSICAL & MOTOR
DEVELOPMENT

CREATIVITY &
THE ARTS

Wake Up!

Act it out!

1. Have all the children pretend to go to sleep when the lights are turned off.

2. Tell them what they will wake up as when the lights are turned on. For example, "When the lights turn on, you will wake up as a busy bumblebee, flying around looking for pollen. You are surrounded by beautiful flowers. It's a beautiful spring day."

3. When you turn on the lights, the participants will wake up as whatever you instructed. The children can move around the room performing actions that fit with the role you gave them. For example, they can move around as bees collecting pollen.

4. When it's time for the class to go to sleep again, turn off the lights. Remind the children to go to sleep and close their eyes. Ask students who are lying too close to each other to move apart. Sometimes students may accidentally bump into each other, so it's important for them to have some space between themselves and their classmates. When the children are motionless and silent, tell them the next creature they will wake up as.

Encore!

Use what the class is learning about to plan which creatures students will wake up as. If it's Halloween, they can wake up as:

- a bat
- a trick-or-treater
- a witch flying on a broomstick

- a mummy
- a werewolf
- a monster

Spotlight on . . .
PHYSICAL & MOTOR
DEVELOPMENT

Freeze Dance

Materials

○ music

○ masking tape to divide the room in half

Act it out!

1. Have children gathered on one side of the room.

2. Begin by playing music for this classic movement game.

3. While the music is playing, children dance.

4. When the music stops, children have to freeze.

5. If students continue moving when the music stops, they cross to the other side of the room. The children who are on the opposite side of the room can move when the music stops, while the other children dance when the music is playing.

Spotlight on . . .
PHYSICAL & MOTOR
DEVELOPMENT

CREATIVITY &
THE ARTS

Act it out!

1. All participants pretend to be toys that have come alive in a toy shop.

2. All of you will pretend to be different toys together, but when you announce the toy shop owner is coming, all the different toys freeze.

3. When you announce the toy shop owner has left, the different toys come alive again.

Encore!

Here is a list of possible toys that students can play:

- a bouncy ball
- a stuffed rabbit
- an action figure
- a baby doll
- a cowboy
- a piggy bank
- a rocking horse

You can also signal for the toys to freeze by starting and stopping music or by having an adult assistant pretending to be the toy shop owner leave and enter the toy shop. The assistant can even interact with the toys.

There are various good books that take place in a toy shop. Consider reading *Corduroy* by Don Freeman.

Spotlight on . . .
PHYSICAL & MOTOR
DEVELOPMENT

CREATIVITY &
THE ARTS

Sound and Movement

Act it out!

1. Have the children stand in a circle.

2. Perform a sound and movement.

3. Have the class repeat the sound and movement.

4. Go around the circle one at a time, allowing each actor to create a sound and movement that the group repeats. Continue until everyone has had a turn.

Encore!

This can be a great getting-to-know-you game if you have children say their name along with the movement.

Spotlight on . . .
PHYSICAL & MOTOR
DEVELOPMENT

Shape Drawing with the Body
. . . .

Act it out!

1. Tell students to spread out around the classroom until they have enough space to move their outstretched arms without bumping into anyone else.

2. Call out a shape and a body part. Tell the children to draw the shape using that part of their body in their own space.

Encore!

Here are some examples you can draw:

- circles with your arms
- circles with your tummy
- circles with your pinky
- rectangles with your thumb
- rectangles with your big toe
- squares with your elbow

- squares with your knee
- squares with your feet
- triangles with your head
- triangles with your nose
- triangles with your bum

This activity helps loosen up the body and teaches children about shapes.

Spotlight on . . .
PHYSICAL & MOTOR
DEVELOPMENT

COGNITIVE
DEVELOPMENT

Shoe Switcheroo
. . . .

Act it out!

1. Have students walk around the space like they are wearing different shoes.

2. When you turn off the lights, the participants have to freeze in place.

3. Keep the lights off as long as you need for everyone to stand still. Sometimes participants are having so much fun they forget to freeze and need a little more time.

4. When everyone is still, tell the class the next pair of shoes they will pretend to wear while walking around the space.

5. Wait until everyone is still before you turn the lights back on, signaling the students to move forward, pretending to wear a new pair of shoes.

Encore!

Here is a list of different types of shoes children can pretend to wear:

- ballerina slippers
- flip-flops in the sand
- hiking boots
- ice skates
- rain boots

- roller skates
- scuba flippers
- shoes covered in sticky glue on the bottom
- snow boots
- tennis shoes

Spotlight on . . .
PHYSICAL & MOTOR
DEVELOPMENT

CREATIVITY &
THE ARTS

Encourage the children to imagine the different environments they might be in while wearing these shoes. If you want, you can even have them "take off" the different shoes when it's time to put on a new pair.

Instead of turning the lights on and off, you can play and stop music to freeze participants.

Jump like a . . .

Act it out!

1. Have students line up at one end of the classroom.

2. Tell them to hop across the classroom like a frog.

3. When they reach the far end, they will wait for instruction on how to jump next.

4. Come up with a new way for children to cross the classroom each time. Take suggestions from students.

Encore!

Here is a list of different ways children can jump across the classroom:

- as a frog
- as a rabbit
- as a kangaroo
- as a mountain goat
- as a grasshopper

Spotlight on . . .
PHYSICAL & MOTOR
DEVELOPMENT

Hula-Hoop Hike

Materials

○ fun music   ○ Hula-Hoops, one per child

Act it out!

1. Place Hula-Hoops around the classroom or yard, one for each student.

2. Give participants instructions to move to different Hula-Hoops. There can only be one child per Hula-Hoop. When you tell them to cross to a new Hula-Hoop, give them clear instructions for how they are to cross. Possibilities for movements include the following:

- Fly to another Hula-Hoop like a butterfly.
- Gallop to another Hula-Hoop as a horse.
- Tiptoe quietly to another Hula-Hoop as a mouse.
- Hop to another Hula-Hoop as a frog.
- Waddle to another Hula-Hoop like a penguin.

3. Play fun music during the activity.

Spotlight on . . .
PHYSICAL & MOTOR
DEVELOPMENT

Spotlight on . . .
PHYSICAL & MOTOR
DEVELOPMENT

CREATIVITY &
THE ARTS

Silly Hat Walk

Materials

o goofy music

o a bag full of silly hats

Act it out!

1. Give each student a silly hat.

2. Play the music as students walk around the space as the type of character that would wear that silly hat.

3. Stop the music and have everyone switch hats.

4. Have each child try to get a hat they haven't used yet.

Magic Shoe Store

Act it out!

1. Go on an adventure to a magic shoe store!

2. Pantomime putting on magic shoes as a class. They might have buckles, laces, or zippers. Each pair of shoes will make the students do different things, like shoes that make the wearer fly, slip and slide, jump, dance, or wiggle uncontrollably.

3. Walk around in each pair of magic shoes before changing into a new pair.

4. Give each student the opportunity to tell you what a different pair looks like and makes the wearer do.

Spotlight on . . .
PHYSICAL & MOTOR
DEVELOPMENT

CREATIVITY &
THE ARTS

Robot Remote

Materials

o a remote control of some kind

o inventor or scientist costume (optional)

Act it out!

1. Turn into an inventor or a scientist from the future by putting on a costume piece, if you can.

2. Show the children your special remote and tell the children they are robots. You can turn them on using your remote. One button on the remote makes them walk around. One button makes them jump. Another button can turn the robots off.

3. Have the class come up with ideas for what different buttons can do.

Spotlight on . . .
PHYSICAL & MOTOR
DEVELOPMENT

CREATIVITY &
THE ARTS

Materials

○ restful music

Act it out!

1. Have students lie on their backs with plenty of space between them to move their arms and legs.

2. Play restful, peaceful music.

3. Instruct students to perform various movements while on their backs. Movements that can be done on the back include the following:

   • making a snow angel

   • swimming the backstroke in place

   • lying in your bed, pulling the covers up to your chin

   • pretending you are pedaling a bike with your legs

   • breathing in and out deeply like you are blowing up a balloon

   • lying in the sand on a warm beach, with the sun coming down on you

Spotlight on . . .
PHYSICAL & MOTOR
DEVELOPMENT

Brush Off

Act it out!

1. Have students stand in a circle.

2. Tell them to brush various items off their bodies. For example, "Let's brush snow off ourselves. How does the snow feel?" Make sure to brush items off legs, arms, head, and chest, naming all the body parts. "Now I am brushing snow off my hair. Off my shoulders. Off my feet. Off my legs."

3. Consider taking suggestions from the children of various items they could brush off.

4. When it's time to brush a new item off, say, "Now we have brushed all the snow off. Oh no, we are covered in ants. Let's brush the ants off quickly! How do they feel?" Possible things to be brushed off include the following:

   • ants

   • dirt

   • dog hair

   • dust

   • a mouse

   • snowflakes

   • a spider

   • sticky spider webs

Spotlight on . . .
PHYSICAL & MOTOR
DEVELOPMENT

CREATIVITY &
THE ARTS

Crossing to the Shapes

Materials

o shapes of various colors

Act it out!

1. Put different-colored shapes, such as these, around the room:

    • a red triangle   • a green square

    • a blue circle   • a yellow rectangle

2. Tell the actors to walk to the different-colored shapes in different ways:

    • hopping like a bunny   • dancing like a ballerina

    • flying like a butterfly   • jumping like a kangaroo

    • stomping like an elephant

Encore!

You could also teach the children numbers or letters this way. Put the numbers or letters on signs that children walk to.

Spotlight on . . .
PHYSICAL & MOTOR
DEVELOPMENT

APPROACHES TO
LEARNING

Walk the Line

Materials

o fun music

o masking tape

o pictures of animals

Act it out!

1. Using masking tape, create straight lines around the floor of the classroom, between three to five feet in length.

2. Tape pictures of different animals around the classroom, next to the masking tape lines.

3. Allow the students to move around the classroom, taking turns walking on the different lines and pretending to be the different animals as they find them on the lines. Use the music to signify when children should start moving and to let them know when to stop.

Encore!

You can also put children into small groups on the different lines. Let them walk the line several times before switching the groups to a different line.

Spotlight on . . .
PHYSICAL & MOTOR
DEVELOPMENT

Moving with Sheer Scarves

Sheer scarves are a great investment for creative movement. Many creative movement activities, as well as other activities throughout this book, are enhanced through the use of sheer scarves. Try introducing scarves to activities such as the "Freeze Dance" (page 88) or the "Circle Dance" (page 57).

Here are other various movements you and the children can perform using scarves:

- Play peekaboo using scarves.
- Pretend the scarf is blowing in a gentle breeze, then a strong wind, then a heavy storm.
- Pretend the scarf is like a leaf falling from a tree.
- Pretend the scarf is like a bird flying through the air.
- Imagine the scarf is a pet, such as a dog on a walk.
- Turn your scarf into a superhero cape.
- Turn your scarf into a peacock's tail.
- Turn your scarf into a dishcloth and pretend to wash imaginary dishes.
- Pretend your scarf is a bonnet for an elderly woman.
- Use the scarf as protection from the rain.
- Use the scarf as a blanket.
- Use the scarf as an apron.
- Slither your scarf along the ground like a snake.
- Twirl your scarf like a helicopter propeller.
- Move your scarf like a candle's flame.
- Wave your scarf like a flag.
- Move your scarf like a caterpillar climbing up the wall.
- Swish your scarf like a horse's tail.
- Swing your scarf like an elephant's trunk.
- Form your scarf into a ball, with a little left out like a tail, and make it swim like a fish.
- Ball the scarf up, throw it up in the air, and catch it like a ball.
- Move the scarf like a shooting star.
- Move the scarf like a rainbow.
- Move the scarf like clouds.
- Wear the scarf like a tie.
- Free dance with the scarf.
- When you are finished, you can wave bye-bye to one another with the scarves.

Or using two scarves, you can try the following:

- Flap the scarves like butterfly wings.
- Flutter the scarves like bee wings.
- Flap the scarves like chicken wings.
- Fly with the scarves like an airplane.
- Pretend the scarves are like flowers blowing in the wind.
- Pretend the scarves are like leaves on tree branches.
- Pretend the scarves are like leaves falling down.
- Imagine the scarves are like snow drifting down.
- Wad up the scarves and throw them like snowballs.
- Hold the scarves to the head like pigtails.
- Hold the scarves to the head like elephant ears.

You can also invite children to draw various shapes in the air using the sheer scarves.

Explore moving the scarves in different directions and at different tempos:

- left, right
- up, down
- high, low
- fast, slow

Below are examples of activities that can be played with or without scarves.

Name Dance

Materials

○ two scarves per child (optional)

Act it out!

1. Have children stand in a circle. Start off by saying, "We are doing the '[Your Name] Dance.'"

2. Show the class the gesture, using the scarves if available. The gesture can be as simple as raising the scarf up and down.

3. Have everyone dance by doing your gesture.

4. Now the children will learn a new dance. One at a time, have each child come up with a movement or gesture. It can be jumping, moving his arm up and down, or moving his arm in circles. Call the dance "[Child's Name] Dance." For example, "Javier's Dance." Have him perform his move several times for the group. If children need help coming up with a movement, have them ask a friend for help. They can also say, "No, thank you" if they are too nervous to come up with a dance move.

5. When everyone knows the move, say, "Let's do Javier's Dance."

6. Play until everyone who wants a turn inventing a dance move for the class has gotten to play. The students can also perform this activity while moving freely around the room, but make sure you have a strategy in place to get their attention when it's time to move on to the next gesture.

Encore!

Instead of doing dances inspired by the children, you can also lead the class in dances inspired by animals or characters. For example:

- the ballerina dance
  - the butterfly dance
  - the chicken dance
  - the cricket dance
  - the frog dance
  - the huge giant dance
  - the kangaroo dance
  - the lion dance

Spotlight on . . .
PHYSICAL & MOTOR
DEVELOPMENT

Knee Dance

Materials

- two scarves per child (optional)

Act it out!

1. Have students stand in a circle.

2. Tell them they are going to do a dance involving their knees. Tell them they may move their arms and their scarves however they wish while they do the knee dance:
   - Knock your knees together.
   - Bend them up and down.
   - Wiggle your knees.
   - Keep your knees straight and move side to side.
   - Bend your knees into a plié like a ballerina.
   - Move both of your knees in a circle.
   - Draw circles with one knee, then switch and draw circles with the other knee.
   - Stand like a flamingo with one knee bent; switch knees.
   - Take a huge jump, bending your knees.

Encore!

You can also create dances using other parts of the body, such as an elbow dance.

Spotlight on . . .
PHYSICAL & MOTOR
DEVELOPMENT

CREATIVITY &
THE ARTS

Familiar Favorites

Sheep and Shepherd

· ·

Materials

- a rope (optional)

- costume pieces (optional)

- nighttime soundscape or peaceful music (optional)

Act it out!

1. Begin with one child, or the teacher for the first round, as the shepherd and the rest of the children as sheep. The sheep are in a field at night and want to stay up a little later, but the shepherd is rounding them up for bed.

2. When the shepherd isn't looking, the sheep can move. If the shepherd catches a sheep moving, the sheep walks around, following the shepherd around the space and mimicking the shepherd's movements. The sheep could also grab onto a rope that the shepherd holds, or the shepherd can put the sheep to sleep in the pen. Blinking, breathing heavily, or shaking do not count as movement, as they are involuntary. You may need to remind shepherds that they have to actually see students move, not just notice that they have moved while their backs are turned. You may also add that the shepherd will catch a sheep if he is too loud. Still, it's fun for students to "baa" a little bit as sheep, so implement this policy only if the baaing is so loud it's distracting.

3. Play until there is one sheep left. That last sheep becomes the new shepherd.

Encore!

Consider turning down the lights and playing music, or nighttime sounds, such as crickets chirping. Give the shepherd a flashlight to shine around the space.

You could also play this game as an explorer finding magical creatures in an enchanted forest. Children can pretend to be creatures such as fairies, dragons, or other fantastical animals. Or the shepherd could be a zookeeper trying to find animals that have escaped from their cages. The shepherd can also be a guard in a museum where the statues come alive at night. Feel free to adapt the game to your classroom's interests. Also, allowing children to dress up as their characters, such as mythical creatures, animals, or a statue, helps them get into character and is extremely fun for children. If possible, allow time for them to share the character they created.

Spotlight on . . .
PHYSICAL & MOTOR
DEVELOPMENT

CREATIVITY &
THE ARTS

Act it out!

1. Get children into a line.

2. The person at the front of the line will be the leader. Be the leader first so they can follow your example.

3. The rest of the students will follow the leader's movements exactly.

4. Let the students each have a turn being the leader.

Encore!

Put the students in small groups and let them be a flock of birds flying around the space (see "Follow the Flock" on page 69). The rest of the flock needs to follow the leader of the flock.

Spotlight on . . .
PHYSICAL & MOTOR
DEVELOPMENT

Simon Says

Act it out!

1. Have students stand in a line, facing Simon. You will begin as Simon, modeling how to play the game. When children understand the game, consider letting them be Simon for short turns.

2. Simon will tell the class to do specific actions. Simon has to use the phrase "Simon says" for the class to follow his instructions. If Simon doesn't say, "Simon says," the students don't have to do the action. For example, if Simon says, "Simon says cluck like a chicken," then students should cluck like a chicken. But if Simon says, "Cluck like a chicken," the students don't have to do it.

Encore!

Choose actions in Simon Says that reflect the theme being explored that day in class. For example, if the theme is the season of fall, then the leader can say, "Simon says hold out your arms and spread out your fingers like tree branches full of red, yellow, or brown leaves. Simon says sway your arms, like branches blowing in the wind. Simon says let your fingers fall to the ground like leaves falling from a tree. Simon says rake up the leaves in front of you to make a huge pile."

Let the children take turns being Simon.

If children move when Simon didn't say to, remind them, "Simon didn't say to," but don't count them out.

You don't have to say "Simon says." It can be "[your name] says" or a silly made-up name.

You can also play the game using a puppet named Simon who facilitates the game.

Spotlight on . . .
PHYSICAL & MOTOR
DEVELOPMENT

COGNITIVE
DEVELOPMENT

Act it out!

1. One person is a stoplight while the rest of the participants try to tag her.

2. Participants stand in a horizontal line at least ten feet away from the stoplight.

3. When the stoplight says, "Green light," the participants go, moving toward the stoplight. When the stoplight says, "Red light," the participants must stop moving.

4. If the stoplight catches someone moving during a red light, that child goes back to the beginning.

5. If a child reaches and touches the stoplight, start a new round by letting him be the stoplight and having all other participants go back to the beginning.

6. Use a new movement to cross the room each round. The possibilities are as endless as your class's imagination, so ask them for suggestions. Instead of having children run, encourage them to do different actions, such as these:

   - hop like bunny rabbits
   - leap like gazelles
   - walk like elephants
   - fly like butterflies
   - waddle like penguins
   - dance like ballerinas
   - move like the floor is covered in Jell-O
   - move like the floor is covered in ice
   - move like the floor is covered in sticky glue
   - be grumpy bears
   - be chickens
   - move with giant steps
   - move with baby steps
   - gallop like horses
   - crawl like babies

You can also choose actions that match what the students are learning about in class. For example, if it's winter they can cross as if:

- they are on ice skates;
- the floor is covered in a foot of snow;
- it's freezing cold; or
- they are pulling a sled through the snow.

Spotlight on . . .
PHYSICAL & MOTOR
DEVELOPMENT

CREATIVITY &
THE ARTS

CHAPTER EIGHT

. . . .

Cooldowns, Reflection Tools, and Closing Rituals

Cooldown Activities

A cooldown activity helps children transition to the reflection and closing ritual. The activity can be short, just a few minutes. The cooldown gives children the space to transition from a high-energy activity where they were moving freely to a group activity that is more focused and together. Breathing activities found on pages 24–29 and yoga activities on pages 44–45 are strong choices for cooldown activities. Playing calming music, like classical guitar music or a soundscape of the ocean, can help create a serene, contemplative atmosphere during the cooldown. An essential oil diffuser with calming scents such as lavender can also help children transition into the cooldown.

Act it out!

1. Have the class stand in a circle facing each other.

2. Stretch up high.

3. Stretch down low.

4. Stretch to the right.

5. Stretch to the left.

6. Lie down on your back and stretch out your whole body.

7. Make a snow angel while on your back.

8. Turn over and stretch like a cat.

Yawn!

Act it out!

1. Have children sit or stand in a circle.

2. Tell them, "We are going to yawn as a class. Breathe in and open your mouth nice and big and let out a yawn. Stretch your arms upward. Yawn again, nice and big. This time pat your mouth while you yawn."

3. Yawn several times. Consider yawning like different animals, such as a lion, house cat, or snake.

Plant a Tree

Act it out!

1. Have children stand in a circle.

2. Tell them, "We are going to be seeds that grow into beautiful trees. Curl up like a seed. Now imagine that the warm sun is shining down on you. The rain is falling onto the ground. Now, let's begin to grow. Let's reach through the soil. Let's rise upward. Let's spread out our branches and get lots of sunlight." As the seeds grow, you will slowly stand. You will end the activity stretched out as far as you can, arms outstretched.

Porcupine

. . . .

Act it out!

1. Have children lie on their backs, spread out from each other.

2. Tell them, "You are a porcupine. When I say curl up, you will curl up your body as tightly as possible. When I say stretch out, you will stretch out your body as big as you can."

3. Instruct them to curl up and stretch out several times.

Yoga Poses

. . . .

Act it out!

1. Downhill Skier Pose:

   • Place feet together, firmly planted to the earth.

   • Next, bend your knees and sweep your arms back.

2. Snowboarder Pose (Warrior II Pose):

   • One leg is bent at the knee, the other stretched out behind you. The foot of the leg that's behind you should be turned horizontally.

   • Your torso is twisted; the snowboarder's arms are stretched out horizontally.

   • Take deep breaths of the fresh mountain air.

3. Ice Skater (Warrior III Pose):

   • One leg is firmly planted on the ground.

   • Next, stretch one leg back, hands extended in front of you.

Yoga Under the Sea

. . . .

Act it out!

1. Diver Pose (Superhuman Pose):

   • Lie on the ground on your tummy and bring your arms up in front of you like a diver.

   • Lift your feet up, diving into the ocean.

2. Dolphin Pose:

   • Now flap your arms and tail (feet), becoming a dolphin swimming in the ocean.

3. Seal Pose (Cobra Pose):

   • Now, with your legs straight out behind you, arch your back so your chest is directed upward.

• Bring your flippers (arms) together like a seal.

4. Swimmer Stretch:

   • Then, lie on your back.

   • Move your arms and legs as though you are doing a backstroke in place.

5. Starfish Stretch:

   • Stretch your arms and legs apart as wide as you can.

   • Breathe in through your nose, then breathe out like you are blowing giant bubbles under the sea.

A Spring Day Cooldown

1. Have children sit in a circle.

2. Tell them to imagine they are planting a seed in the ground in front of them.

3. Have children bring their fingers down like spring rain onto their garden.

4. Students turn their hands into a circle, like a sun overhead, to warm their garden.

5. They turn their hands into birds, flying over their garden.

6. They make their fingers into flowers growing up from the ground.

7. The students breathe in deeply to smell all the beautiful flowers they have planted in their garden.

Summer Fun Cooldown

1. Have the children sit in a circle.

2. Tell the children to roll their shoulders backward three times and then forward three times, slowly and gently.

3. Have the children breathe in and put their arms up in a circle, like the sun rising.

4. When the children breathe out, the sun sets as they move their arms to the floor in front of them, still connected in a circle.

5. Tell the students to pantomime licking a popsicle.

6. Have them move their arms like they are swimming at the pool.

7. Instruct the students to lie down and move their legs as though they are riding a bike, slowly.

8. Have them breathe in, imagining that their tummy is a beach ball expanding. When they breathe out, tell them to breathe out like the wind blowing over the ocean.

1. Have the class sit in a circle.

2. As the students inhale deeply, they lift their arms up like tree branches.

3. When they breathe out, they lower their arms like gently falling leaves. Repeat.

4. Have children breathe in through their noses deeply, raising their arms over their heads.

5. Then they release their breath through their mouths and their teeth to make a noise like wind in the trees when they exhale.

6. The students can even wave their arms over their heads with extended fingers like tree branches in the wind when they exhale.

7. Put your hands together to make a bird. Have everyone use their hands to make a flock of Canadian geese, migrating for the winter.

8. Lift your arms up and breathe in, then move them down and breathe out, like your arms are bird wings. Repeat several times until the children's bodies are calm.

Winter Wonderland Cooldown

1. Have the students lie down on the floor with plenty of space between them so they don't accidentally bump into one another.

2. Make snow angels on the floor. Breathe in when your arms and legs go up, and breathe out when your arms and legs go down.

3. Then, have the children sit up and make a circle as a class, like they are warming their hands around a fire on a cold winter night.

4. Tell them to breathe in like they are smelling the delicious soup on the fire, then out like they are blowing on a hot bowl of soup. Have them do this a few times. You can even pretend to eat the soup.

5. Have the children do a deep yawn and stretch. They can imagine that they are snuggling into a warm sleeping bag, and close their eyes. Hum them a lullaby.

6. Tell them that when you ring your bell, they should sit up in a circle by the count of ten so you can all return to the classroom.

Reflection Activities

It's important to give children a moment to reflect on and process their experiences after drama class. Reflection isn't only summarizing the main events of an activity but an opportunity to process and analyze an experience (Epstein 2003, 2). A short reflection time allows children to make observations, express interests, and articulate their feelings about the day's drama activities. Reviewing their experience and articulating their intentions helps young children develop a sense of responsibility for themselves and the choices they make (Epstein 2003, 8).

Allowing children to express their experiences also develops introspection and language skills, as well as enhances the learning of what topics were explored in drama class. According to the noted National Research Council report, *Eager to Learn: Educating Our Preschoolers*, metacognitive skill development, or thinking about one's own thinking, "allows children to learn to solve problems more effectively" (2001, 10). Ask children genuine, open-ended questions that explore their intentions and experiences, not questions to which you already know the answer (Epstein 2003, 5). Praise can end the conversation, but listening, commenting, recording children's ideas, and asking questions promotes reflection (Epstein 2003, 5). This is also a time for you as a teacher to receive feedback about what was working for the class and what students might like to do differently. Make sure to include some kind of brief reflection after each drama class.

Closing Circle Time

Act it out!

1. Class begins and ends with students seated or standing in a circle, facing each other. Here is a list of questions you could ask students during a closing circle time:

   • What did you enjoy about drama today?

   • What questions did you have?

   • What made you smile today?

   • What would you like to do more of?

   • What did another classmate do well?

   • What would you like to learn more about?

Materials

o phone or video camera

o television or smartboard

Act it out!

1. Record part of the drama or dramatic play session with your phone or video camera.

2. Project the final result for the class to watch.

3. Briefly discuss the children's feelings and observations about their performance.

   • What did they see while watching themselves?

   • What did they like about their performance?

   • What would they have done differently?

   • Do they have any affirmations for their classmates?

Breaking News!

Act it out!

1. As teacher-in-role, pretend to be a news reporter, reporting live from your preschool or child care center.

2. Interview each child about how she felt about the day's drama class, as though you are reporting the news on TV. What did the children enjoy? What was their favorite part of class?

Encore!

Ask an assistant or coteacher to be your camera person, pretending to record the interviews.

One-Word Reflection

Act it out!

1. Have each child stand in the circle.

2. One at a time, ask each student to say one word to describe the day.

Make a Face

Act it out!

1. Have the children stand or sit in a circle.

2. Each child uses facial expressions to demonstrate how he felt about today's drama class.

Curious Minds

Act it out!

1. Have the children stand or sit in a circle.

2. Every student shares one question she has about the day's drama class.

Curtain Call! End-of-Class Rituals

A closing ritual is an important part of any drama class. A closing ritual creates structure and helps students transition and refocus on what they are doing next in their day. It's important for the children to know that the drama class is finished, so the activities don't continue beyond the drama class and into the next school subject. Using the same activity or activities to finish each class helps establish such a ritual and reminds children that the drama class is coming to a close.

End-of-Drama-Class Song

Act it out!

1. Create a song using a familiar tune. Below are examples of two songs to the tune of *Mary Had a Little Lamb*:

> In drama class we laugh and play,
> Laugh and play, laugh and play.
> Now that drama is done today,
> We will say good-bye.

Or

> Drama class is done today,
> Done today, done today.
> We danced, imagined, laughed, and played,
> But now it's time for snack
>   [or whatever activity is next].

Bubble Blowing

Materials

o bubble mixture and wand

Act it out!

1. Blow bubbles for your students at the end of class as a visual indication that it's finished.

Encore! Take a Bow

Act it out!

1. Have all the students stand in a circle.

2. Each child bows, one at a time, while the others applaud her.

3. Take a final bow together as a class.

4. Give each other a final round of applause by clapping hands while moving them in a circle.

Wave Good-bye

Act it out!

1. Stand in a circle.

2. Have everyone wave good-bye to each student one at a time, stating his or her name as you move around the circle.

   Teacher: Let's wave good-bye to Jamal.

   Everyone: Good-bye, Jamal!

   Teacher: Let's wave good-bye to Vashti.

   Everyone: Good-bye, Vashti!

Handshakes

Act it out!

1. Have all the students stand in two lines.

2. Have the children shake hands and congratulate each other as they go down the line, similar to how athletes shake hands after a game.

Familiar Favorites

This is a popular fingerplay in many early childhood classrooms that can also be employed by drama educators at the end of drama class.

Gotta Fly, Butterfly!

. . . .

Act it out!

1. Sit or stand in a circle.

2. Come up with a gesture or fingerplay for each different phrase. You can do this as a class the first day, or you can create the gesture or fingerplay and teach it to the class.

3. Use the same fingerplay each class to create a class ritual.

   - See you later, alligator! (Move arms up and down like alligator jaws, with the fingers curled and separated like teeth.)
   - After a while, crocodile! (Move arms like a crocodile swimming through water, or chomp their teeth like a crocodile chomping.)
   - See you soon, raccoon! (Give yourself a raccoon mask with two fingers around each eye.)
   - Gotta fly, butterfly! (Put hands together and move fingers like butterfly wings.)
   - Shut the door, dinosaur! (Pretend to push a door shut.)
   - Hit the road, toad! (Hop two fingers around like a tiny toad if seated; hop like a toad if standing.)
   - Toodle-oo, kangaroo! (Hop like a kangaroo if standing.)
   - Take care, koala bear! (Pretend to climb with hands, or have fingers climb up arm like a koala bear.)
   - Blow a kiss, goldfish! (Give yourself gills with hands on either side of face, while blowing out cheeks.)
   - Here's a hug, ladybug! (Give yourself a hug.)
   - Gotta go, buffalo! (Give yourself horns, with two fingers like a buffalo.)
   - Gotta scoot, newt! (Have your fingers crawl slowly like a newt up your arm.)
   - Ta-ta for now, cow! (Pretend to chew cud while waving to each other.)

PART THREE

Incorporating
Music, Art, and
Literature into the
Drama Classroom

CHAPTER NINE

Incorporating Music

Music is an important component of a drama class, and there are a variety of ways you can incorporate musical experiences to enhance a drama class. Playing music during a theatre activity, especially a creative movement activity, establishes a mood and can inspire children to move in expressive ways. Stopping and starting music is a great way to signal to a class that an activity is starting or ending. Singing directions to a theatre game is a great way to get children's attention and incorporate singing into a drama class. Creating drama activities based off children's favorite songs enhances children's enjoyment of their favorite tunes.

Incorporating Musical Instruments

Musical instruments can be incorporated into a drama class in a variety of ways. You can use them to gain the attention of the children during drama class. You can play a kazoo, hit a meditation gong, or play a short tune on the recorder to signify the beginning or end of class (this can become part of your class ritual). You can use a variety of instruments during creative movement activities to add to the fun, such as a variety of shakers (egg shakers are great because they don't get too loud) or add bells to elastic bands that children can wear on their wrists and ankles.

Types of Musical Instruments Recommended for a Pre-K Classroom

Below is a list of instruments that young children can use during drama class. Most of these are percussive instruments that are useful for creating rhythms together:

- tambourines
- maracas
- triangles and beaters
- castanets
- rain sticks
- handbells
- zills or finger cymbals
- chime bars
- scrapers

Create Your Own!

Children can also create their own musical instruments. Allow children to string bells onto pipe cleaners or elastic to wear around their ankles and wrists. Children can create their own tambourines and maracas using dried seeds and beans and recyclables, such as old yogurt containers with their lids taped or glued down or decorated paper plates stapled together by a teacher.

Activities Using Musical Instruments

Listen Up!

Materials

- kazoo or noisemaker

Act it out!

Use a funny noisemaker or kazoo at the beginning and end of an activity to signify that the activity is starting or stopping. You can also play the instrument when you need the children to focus on you.

Director's note

This activity could be used as a centering activity during drama class.

Conductor

Materials

○ various musical instruments, such as the following:

- bells

- tambourine

- rhythm sticks

- drum

- kazoo

- any other instruments you have handy

Act it out!

1. Have four to six children sit in a row.

2. One child will be the conductor. (You may need to be the conductor first to demonstrate the game.)

3. The seated children are the musicians. Give each child a musical instrument.

4. When the conductor gently touches a musician's head, the musician is allowed to start playing her instrument. When the conductor gently touches the musician's head again, the musician will have to stop making noise. The conductor can have all musicians playing at once or playing one at a time.

5. If the conductor wants the group to get louder, he should raise his hands high. If he wants them to play softer, he should put his hands to the ground.

6. Let each student have a turn as a conductor and as a musician.

Encore!

For a similar activity, see "Sound Effects Story" on page 168.

Director's note

This activity could be used as an imaginative play activity during drama class.

Spotlight on . . .
SOCIAL & EMOTIONAL
LEARNING

Walk to the Beat

Materials

○ a percussive instrument, such as a drum

Act it out!

1. Actors walk from one end of the classroom to another, walking to the beat of the drum played by the teacher.

- Let the children explore walking with different rhythms, such as walking to the teacher playing a steady beat or an uneven beat.

- Explore beating the drum fast, causing the children to walk quickly. Then play the drum slowly, letting the children walk slowly. As you play, gradually change the tempo or quickly change the tempo to let the children explore gradually or quickly walking faster or slower.

- Play the drum with varying volume and energy. Perhaps at one point it's hard and loud and later on the beat is gentle and soft. This will let the children explore how their movement changes based on the drum beats' varying volume and energy.

- Throughout the activity, stop playing the drum abruptly so that children have to listen attentively to come to a complete stop.

Director's note

This activity could be used as a creative movement activity during drama class.

Can You Play That Rhythm?

* *

Materials

○ various musical instruments, such as shakers or handbells on elastic bands, one for each child

Act it out!

1. Stand or sit in a circle, facing each other.

2. Place one of the various instruments in front of each child. Say the name of the instrument as you set it down. Maybe use an adjective that alliterates with the first letter of the word, like "beautiful bells" or "terrific tambourine." Giving everyone the same instrument, like egg shakers, is also a strong choice.

3. Do a dance move and play a simple rhythm for the children. Let them pick up their instruments and try to imitate the dance move and rhythm.

4. See if they can repeat it back to you.

5. Do this several times, then allow the children who wish to, to create rhythms individually for the group to repeat.

Director's note

This activity could be used as a creative movement activity during drama class.

Spotlight on . . .
PHYSICAL & MOTOR
DEVELOPMENT

Spotlight on . . .
PHYSICAL & MOTOR
DEVELOPMENT

Materials

o various musical instruments

Act it out!

1. Have children stand in a circle facing one another. Make sure that they have plenty of space. If you have the space, you can also allow the children to move freely around the area.

2. Tell them what animal they will pretend to be before playing the instrument. Remind them that they can act like the animal while you are playing, but they must stop moving when you stop playing the instrument.

3. The children will pretend to be different animals while you play different instruments.

4. When you stop playing the instrument, the students will stop moving.

5. After you have played the instrument, tell them the name of the instrument that you played. Here is a list of instruments that sound like animal noises you can use for this activity:

   • Shake a maraca or shaker and pretend to be rattlesnakes.

   • Blow a duck call and pretend to be ducks.

   • Play a recorder or small mouth pipe and pretend to be birds.

   • Play a large drum and pretend to be huge stomping elephants.

   • Play a rain stick and pretend to be playing in a rainstorm.

   • Play a bell and pretend to be fairies.

   • Honk a bike horn and pretend to be cars, or lie on your backs and pretend to be riding bikes.

Encore!

Consider displaying photos of the various animals or objects you call out, or project their images onto a smartboard. The children can also take turns playing the different instruments.

Director's note

This activity could be used as an imaginative play activity during drama class.

Spotlight on . . .
PHYSICAL & MOTOR
DEVELOPMENT

CREATIVITY &
THE ARTS

Materials

o egg shakers, drums, or other percussive instruments, one per child (optional)

Act it out!

1. Divide children into pairs. Have them sit cross-legged across from each other.

2. Give each pair instruments, or instruct them to create rhythms by clapping or patting their laps.

3. Have one child create a short rhythm and his partner try to mimic his rhythm. Have partners switch roles to make sure every child has the opportunity to create a rhythm and to try and replicate their partner's rhythm.

Encore!

You can also do this activity as a class and have the entire class try to repeat the rhythm a child or the teacher has created.

Director's note

This activity could be used as a warm-up during drama class.

Spotlight on . . .
COGNITIVE
DEVELOPMENT

Story Time Sound Effects

Add musical instruments that children can play during specific moments in a story. Play instruments when the main character's name is said or a repetitive phrase is used. You can also create a short song that you sing at certain times in the story, such as whenever you say a certain word or phrase. Below is an example of this activity with the book *Chicka Chicka Boom Boom*.

Materials

o various percussive instruments, such as hand shakers, one per child

o *Chicka Chicka Boom Boom* by Bill Martin Jr. and John Archambault

Act it out!

1. Tell the children you are going to read a book titled *Chicka Chicka Boom Boom*. When they hear the phrase "Chicka, chicka, boom, boom," they can shake their shakers.

2. Give the children their shakers.

3. Read the book *Chicka Chicka Boom Boom* by Bill Martin Jr. and John Archambault.

4. The children shake their shakers whenever you say, "Chicka, chicka, boom, boom."

Spotlight on . . .
LANGUAGE &
LITERACY

Director's note

This activity could be used as an imaginative play activity during drama class.

Create Musical Dramas Using Popular Children's Songs

Children enjoy incorporating songs they like and are familiar with into drama class. You can bring familiar songs to life for children by dramatizing them or doing activities inspired from these songs. You can sing a familiar tune and tell children to name that song to get their attention throughout class. You can sing short songs as part of class rituals. Here are some popular songs that you can use to create theatre activities:

- "Baa, Baa, Black Sheep"
- "Have You Seen the Muffin Man"
- "Hey Diddle Diddle"
- "I've Been Working on the Railroad"
- "Jingle Bells"
- "Little Bo Peep"
- "Mary Had a Little Lamb"

Drama Activities Based on Popular Children's Songs

Row, Row, Row Your Boat

Act it out!

1. Have children sit in rows like they are rowing a large boat. Be the boat's captain at the back of the boat.

2. Let the children act out rowing a boat while they sing the song "Row, Row, Row Your Boat."

> Row, row, row your boat,
> gently down the stream.
> Merrily, merrily, merrily, merrily,
> life is but a dream.

3. Have the students dock at various places down the stream, like a beautiful meadow, near a waterfall, or by a herd of deer (have them pretend to be deer). They could also dock their boat along various coastlines on different islands, such as Antarctica, Australia, or Hawaii. You could even row your boats to imaginary places such as Candy Land or a new island never discovered before. Each time the class rows to a new place, sing the song "Row, Row, Row Your Boat." Children can get out of the boat to explore the different environments or just discuss what they see.

Director's note

This activity could be used as an imaginative play activity during drama class.

Spotlight on . . .
CREATIVITY &
THE ARTS

Act it out!

1. Sing the song "Old MacDonald Had a Farm."

> Old MacDonald had a farm, E-I-E-I-O
> And on his farm he had a cow, E-I-E-I-O
> With a moo, moo here and a moo, moo there
> Here a moo, there a moo
> Everywhere a moo, moo
> Old MacDonald had a farm, E-I-E-I-O

You can add verses, such as these:

- pig (oink, oink)
- duck (quack, quack)
- chicken (cluck, cluck)
- sheep (baa, baa)
- horse (neigh, neigh)

2. One child, who will be Old MacDonald, leaves the classroom.

3. Divide the other students into different groups of animals on the farm, such as cows, pigs, sheep, horses, or chickens. Each group pretends to be its assigned animal.

4. Old MacDonald comes back into the classroom and tries to guess which animal each group is pretending to be.

5. After Old MacDonald has guessed all the different animals, you should help her feed the animals and put them to bed.

6. Sing a lullaby to the animals, such as "Twinkle, Twinkle, Little Star."

7. Then tell the rooster to crow by making a loud *cock-a-doodle doo*, and tell everyone they can wake up to play again or to move on to the next activity.

Director's note

This activity could be used as an imaginative play activity during drama class.

Spotlight on . . .
CREATIVITY &
THE ARTS

Materials

○ chairs, one per child

Act it out!

1. Sing the song "The Wheels on the Bus."

> The wheels on the bus go round and round,
> round and round,
> round and round.
> The wheels on the bus go round and round,
> all through the town!

You can add additional verses, such as these:

- the people (go up and down)
- the horn (goes beep, beep, beep)
- the wipers (go swish, swish, swish)
- the signals (go blink, blink, blink)
- the motor (goes zoom, zoom, zoom)
- the babies (go waa, waa, waa)
- the parents (go shh, shh, shh)

2. Have the children sit in a line or arrange the chairs in a row, like the inside of a bus. Sit at the front of the line and pretend to be a bus driver, driving the bus.

3. Take an imaginary adventure on the bus. Stop the bus in different places, such as the library, the museum, the park, or the swimming pool. Have kids get out and pretend to visit each place. Take suggestions of where they would like to go.

4. As you travel between destinations, ask the children what they see out the window of the bus.

5. When it's time to get off the bus, have everyone get out of the bus to move on to the next activity.

Director's note

This activity could be used as an imaginative play activity during drama class.

Spotlight on . . .
CREATIVITY &
THE ARTS

Incorporating Classical Music

Use classical music to set the mood for various activities. For warm-up, you can play salsa, upbeat jazz, African drums, or samba. For a cooldown, play relaxing guitar music or harp music. You can also create theatre activities inspired by famous pieces of classical music.

Activities Inspired by Classical Music

Musical Moods

Materials

o various sound clips from famous pieces of classical music

Act it out!

1. Play excerpts of classical music.

2. Ask children how the music makes them feel.

3. Tell students to make a face that reflects that feeling.

Encore!

Here are some music pieces you can use; there is no right or wrong answer for how the music makes a child feel. Different people feel different things when they listen to music. The emotion in parentheses is the expected emotion, but again, they are different for everyone.

- "Moonlight Sonata" by Ludwig van Beethoven (sad)
- *Water Music* by George Frideric Handel (happy)
- "Hungarian Rhapsody No. 2" by Franz Liszt (angry)
- *Night on Bald Mountain* by Modest Mussorgsky (fearful)
- "Dance of the Knights" by Sergei Prokofiev (fearful)
- "Nocturne," op. 9, no. 2 by Frédéric Chopin (sad)
- "Pomp and Circumstance," march no. 1, op. 39 by Edward Elgar (celebratory)
- "Air on a G String" by Johann Sebastian Bach (sad)
- "Radetzky March," op. 228 by Johann Strauss Sr. (happy)
- "Tritsch-Tratsch Polka," op. 214 by Johann Strauss II (happy)
- "Marche Slave" by Pyotr Tchaikovsky (curious)

Director's note

This activity could be used as an imaginative play activity during drama class.

Spotlight on . . .
SOCIAL & EMOTIONAL
LEARNING

Carnival of the Animals

Materials

○ *The Carnival of the Animals* by Camille Saint-Saëns

Act it out!

1. Tell the children about *The Carnival of the Animals* by Saint-Saëns. Explain that each piece of music is inspired by a different animal.

2. Play a little bit of each piece of music, and let the class try to guess which animals inspired which movement of the suite.

3. Tell the children which animal inspired each piece of music. Tell them that when the music starts, they can move around the space as that animal. When the music stops, the children must freeze and wait for directions.

4. Let the children move freely around the space as they pretend to be the animal that inspired that particular movement. Below is a list of the animals that inspired each corresponding movement in the suite:

i. royal lions	viii. donkeys
ii. hens and roosters	ix. cuckoo birds
iii. wild horses	x. aviary
iv. tortoises	xi. pianists
v. elephants	xii. fossils, bones, and dinosaurs
vi. kangaroos	xiii. swans
vii. fish and an aquarium	

5. Have pictures of the different animals available to inspire the children about how to move.

Director's note

This activity could be used as a creative movement activity during drama class.

Materials

o square dancing music, such as "Hoe-down" from *Rodeo* by Aaron Copland

o various Western costume pieces

Act it out!

1. Have a square dance. Allow children to dress up as cowboys and cowgirls, wearing bandanas, cowboy hats, boots, or other costume pieces. Don't be afraid to use cowboy lingo like "howdy," "giddyup," "yeehaw," and "pony up."

2. Here are some basic moves, adapted for early childhood, you can teach the class. You can call out a move or allow the students to creatively free dance using these moves on their own. Play the music while the children dance.

   • Circle Left or Circle Right: Everyone should join hands and skip in a circle, as directed.

   • Couples Promenade: Walk with a friend, holding hands.

   • Do-si-do: Dancers cross their arms in front of them and skip, either roaming free or in a circle as a class. Children could also take turns, with one partner standing still while the other circles her. In the original do-si-do move, dancers circle each other, arms crossed, without turning their backs; this might be too complicated for early childhood. Do what you think your community would enjoy and could learn quickly. Just having them cross their arms and skip freely might be the most enjoyable for many young children.

   • Swing: Children link arms with a partner and walk in a circle in the direction you indicate or skip freely around the room.

   • Bow and Curtsy: Let children bow and curtsy to each other at the beginning and end of the square dance.

   • Giddyup: Gallop around like a pony.

Director's note

Adapt these moves to be as complicated as your group can handle. Maybe they can only bow and curtsy to each other, and they spend the rest of the time galloping like ponies. Maybe your students enjoy roaming free and keeping them in a circle isn't a good fit for the group. Maybe when they do the swing move, they can only handle joining arms followed by skipping in pairs around the room instead of making a circle. Adapt this to fit the needs of your group. The simpler you can make the dance move, the better.

   If possible, make sure to dance with a partner the entire time, so you can model how to do the dance moves in case a child forgets and needs to see an example again. This can be challenging because you need to be observant that all the students are being safe with their bodies and their neighbors' bodies. This activity could be used as a creative movement activity during drama class.

Spotlight on . . .
PHYSICAL & MOTOR
DEVELOPMENT

Little Pigs

Materials

o "Who's Afraid of the Big Bad Wolf?" performed by the Henry Hall Orchestra

o *The Three Little Pigs* by James Marshall

Act it out!

1. Read *The Three Little Pigs* by James Marshall.

2. At the end, allow the children to celebrate and dance as pigs while playing "Who's Afraid of the Big Bad Wolf?" Allow children to pretend to be little pigs while dancing to this happy tune. You could even play "Freeze Dance" from page 88.

Director's note

This activity could be used as a creative movement activity during drama class.

Spotlight on . . .
PHYSICAL & MOTOR
DEVELOPMENT

Meow!

Materials

o "*Duetto Buffo di due Gatti*" or "Funny Cats' Duet" by Gioachino Rossini

Act it out!

1. Have children lie around the space, making sure they are a safe distance from each other.

2. Explain to the actors that this piece of music was inspired by cats. Tell the children that when the music starts, they can pretend to be cats stretching. When the music stops, they must freeze and become silent.

3. Play the music. Let them stretch on the floor like cats.

4. You can also guide the children to pretend to do other cat behaviors such as playing with a ball of string.

Encore!

You could even allow students to make cat ears on headbands for a fun costume piece or art component.

Consider doing the yoga poses (pages 44–45) to warm up the spine.

Director's note

This activity could be used as a creative movement activity during drama class.

Spotlight on . . .
CREATIVITY &
THE ARTS

Materials

- ballroom music, such as "The Blue Danube," op. 314 by Johann Strauss II
- various fairy-tale costume pieces, such as crowns, capes, scarves, fairy wings, or elf outfits

Act it out!

1. Allow all the children to dress up in their best fantasy costumes and attend a magical fairy-tale ball.

2. Play ballroom music for them to free dance to or demonstrate how to do simple waltz steps.

3. Teach the class how to bow or curtsy before asking another person to dance with them.

Director's note

This activity could be used as a creative movement activity during drama class.

Spotlight on . . .
CREATIVITY &
THE ARTS

Parade of the Wooden Soldiers

Materials

- "Parade of the Wooden Soldiers" by Arthur Fiedler

Act it out!

1. Have children line up in single file.

2. Demonstrate how to march.

3. Start the music. Instruct the students to march in place.

4. Lead the line in marching around like toy soldiers.

5. Give the children directions, such as *left*, *right*, *stop*, and *go* as they march around the classroom.

Encore!

Here is some other good marching music:

- "Radetzky March," op. 228 by Johann Strauss Sr.
- "Pomp and Circumstance," march no. 1, op. 39 by Edward Elgar

Director's note

This activity could be used as a creative movement activity during drama class.

Spotlight on . . .
CREATIVITY &
THE ARTS

Spotlight on . . .
CREATIVITY &
THE ARTS

Materials

○ "William Tell Overture" from the opera *William Tell* by Gioachino Rossini

Act it out!

1. Tell the children that when the music starts, they can gallop around the space as though they are horses. When the music stops, they must be silent and freeze.

2. Play the music and let the children gallop around as though they are horses that are moving to the gallop-worthy tune.

Director's note

This activity could be used as a creative movement activity during drama class.

Let It Snow

Materials

○ "Waltz of the Snowflakes" from *The Nutcracker* by Pyotr Tchaikovsky

Act it out!

1. Tell the children that this music was inspired by snow falling down.

2. The actors can pretend that their fingertips are snowflakes falling down. They lift their arms up, then bring their hands down like snowflakes falling from the sky.

3. Tell them that when the music starts, they can move as snowflakes. When the music stops, they should freeze in place.

4. Play the music and let children pretend to be snowflakes falling down to the earth while they dance to the music.

Encore!

To add an art component, the students can create snowflakes to dance with. Children could also dance with white ribbons tied to elastic bands or white scarves.

Spotlight on . . .
PHYSICAL & MOTOR
DEVELOPMENT

Director's note

This activity could be used as a creative movement activity during drama class.

Materials

o "Waltz of the Flowers" from *The Nutcracker* by Pyotr Tchaikovsky

o colorful ribbons or scarves (optional)

Act it out!

1. Explain to the children that this piece of music is titled "Waltz of the Flowers." Have them close their eyes and imagine what type of flower they will be. Ask each child if he wants to share what kind of flower he is. The students who want to share can tell the class what kind of flower they are. Tell them that when the music starts, they can move around the space as though they are flowers in the garden.

2. Play the music. Allow the children to move around the space imagining that they are flowers in a garden. If available, give students the option to dance with colorful ribbons tied to elastic bands or with colorful scarves.

Director's note

This activity could be used as a creative movement activity during drama class.

Spotlight on . . .
CREATIVITY &
THE ARTS

Busy Bees

Materials

o "Flight of the Bumblebee" from *The Tale of Tsar Saltan* by Nikolai Rimsky-Korsakov

Act it out!

1. Tell the children that this piece of music was inspired by bumblebees.

2. While the students are still sitting, have them buzz like angry bees, followed by sad bees, then happy bees. Listen to the music. Ask the children how they think the bee in the music feels.

3. Explain to them that when the music starts, they can move like busy bees. When the music stops, tell them to freeze.

4. Play the music again. Allow the children to be bumblebees, flying around the classroom, collecting nectar to make honey.

Director's note

This activity could be used as a creative movement activity during drama class.

Spotlight on . . .
CREATIVITY &
THE ARTS

Materials

- "Rhapsody in Blue" by George Gershwin

- sidewalk chalk and an area of concrete (optional)

- masking tape (optional)

Act it out!

1. If possible, children can use sidewalk chalk to draw train tracks or roads on concrete. You can also create train tracks or roads indoors using masking tape.

2. Tell the class that "Rhapsody in Blue" is a piece of music inspired by a very busy city. Ask the class about what kinds of things in a city "go" or have wheels.

3. Have the children imagine what kind of vehicle or thing that "goes" in the city they would like to be, such as a bus, subway car, taxicab, fire truck, or other vehicle.

4. Tell them that when you play the music, they can move like the vehicle they've chosen. When the music stops, they need to freeze.

5. Play the music. Let the class move around the space as various vehicles on the roads or tracks they have designed.

Encore!

Make a yellow circle, red circle, and green circle from colored construction paper. Talk about how a red light means "stop," a yellow light means "slow down," and a green light means "go." Hold up these signs during the activity to signify when to stop, go, and slow down.

Director's note

This activity could be used as a creative movement activity during drama class.

Spotlight on . . .
CREATIVITY &
THE ARTS

Bedtime

Materials

- "Brahms' Lullaby" by Johannes Brahms

Act it out!

1. Have the children stand in a circle facing one another.

2. Tell them they will pretend to get ready for bed. Ask them to list some of the things they do before they go to bed.

3. Play the lullaby and pantomime getting ready for bed, such as brushing teeth, putting on pajamas, or reading a goodnight story.

4. The students lie down and imagine being in bed, pulling up the covers to their chins, snuggling down for a good night's sleep.

Encore!

You could also do this activity after playing with a parachute and use the parachute as the covers the children snuggle under.

Director's note

This activity could be used as a cooldown activity during drama class.

The Four Seasons

Materials

- *The Four Seasons* by Antonio Vivaldi

Act it out!

1. Explain to the children that the music was inspired by the different seasons. Ask them what the different seasons are.

2. Tell them you will play "Spring" first. Ask the class what the weather is like on a beautiful spring day. Birds are singing. Flowers are blooming. The class can imagine they are in a beautiful garden.

3. Children can move around when you play the music, and when you stop the music, they need to freeze.

4. Play "Spring" from *The Four Seasons* and let the students move around the space as though they are in a garden on a beautiful spring day.

5. Let them pretend to move around in all the different seasons.

Encore!

Read the book *I Am a Bunny* by Ole Risom or another book about the seasons before doing the activity.

You could also show the class photographs or paintings that take place during each season.

Director's note

This activity could be used as a creative movement activity during drama class.

Spotlight on . . .
CREATIVITY &
THE ARTS

Spotlight on . . .
APPROACHES TO
LEARNING

Candy Land!

Materials

o "Dance of the Sugar Plum Fairy" from *The Nutcracker* by Pyotr Tchaikovsky

Act it out!

1. Tell the children that the music takes place in a candy land. Ask them what a candy land would look like.

2. Tell the children that when you play the music, the class will move as though they are in a candy land. When the music stops, everyone will freeze.

3. Play the music and let the students imagine they are in a candy land. Ask them what they are doing and what they see in the candy land.

Director's note

This activity could be used as an imaginative play activity during drama class.

Peter and the Wolf

Materials

o *Peter and the Wolf* by Sergei Prokofiev

Act it out!

1. This is a wonderful classic to dramatize. Explain to the children that each character has its own theme song featuring a different musical instrument in the orchestra:

   • Peter is represented by the string section.

   • Grandfather is played by the bassoon.

   • The bird is represented by the flute.

   • The duck is played by the oboe.

   • The cat is represented by the clarinet.

   • The wolf is played by the French horn.

   • The hunters are represented by the timpani.

2. Play the different characters' theme songs that are part of the introduction. Let the children move around the space as the different characters as you play the theme music.

3. Listen to the different parts of the story. Here are some ways you can help bring the story to life:

   • Let the children act out dramatic moments in the story.

- Tell the students to make a face that shows how a character is feeling at an emotional part in the story. For example, ask, "What do you think Peter is feeling right now? Can you show me with your face?"
- The class can act out what various characters are doing in the story. "Can you swim like the duck?" "Can you walk through the forest like the hunter?"
- Encourage the children to make up dialogue or monologues for the characters. For example, ask, "What do you think the hunters are saying to each other? What is the wolf thinking right now?"
- Come up with a different action for each character. For example, children can move their arms like wings to represent the character of the bird. Instruct the class to perform the specific action every time the name of that character is mentioned. Allow children to act out the different characters and scenes in the story.

Director's note

This activity could be used as an imaginative play activity during drama class.

Spotlight on . . .
CREATIVITY &
THE ARTS

Musical Children's Books

. . . .

Materials

- *Zin! Zin! Zin! A Violin* by Lloyd Moss

Act it out!

1. Read *Zin! Zin! Zin! A Violin* by Lloyd Moss.

2. Have the children stand in a circle facing one another.

3. Show the class a picture of an instrument in the book, such as a piano. Ask the children how to play a piano. Pantomime as a class how to play a piano.

4. Go through the book and pantomime all the different instruments as a group.

Encore!

Another good music book for young children is *Jazz Baby* by Lisa Wheeler.

Director's note

This activity could be used as a creative movement activity during drama class.

Spotlight on . . .
COGNITIVE
DEVELOPMENT

APPROACHES TO
LEARNING

CHAPTER TEN

. . . .

Incorporating Visual Art

Visual art and drama can be combined to help children explore the theme they are learning that day—such as the season of winter, shapes, or numbers—through both mediums. Children can create these visual art projects while in the art center, or you can reserve a part of drama class for children to create sets, props, costumes, puppets, or reflective drawings. Or children can engage in imaginative play and creative movement activities during drama class that are inspired by famous paintings they are learning about in art class. You can also incorporate what the children are making in art class into their drama center, such as making puppets and a cardboard box puppet stage in the art center and then placing it in the drama center to let the children explore performing with the puppets during their dramatic playtime.

Incorporating Visual Art Projects into Drama Class

Visual art is a great way to first ignite or expand young people's imaginations for drama. Through creating costuming pieces, children can further create and understand their characters. Creating sets and props will help children further reflect on what the environment is like in their drama. Allowing young children to create their own puppets can inspire them to create plays together using their characters. Creating visual artwork after a drama class will engender children to reflect on their experiences, as well as build upon the topic they explored in drama class. This will also give children more ownership over drama class.

Costuming

Allow children to create costume pieces they can wear during a dramatic play session, such as the following:

- sailor hats made of folded paper
- a robot costume made by placing recycled lids on cardboard boxes with string straps
- Robin Hood hats made of folded paper
- crowns the children decorate themselves
- animal ears glued on a headband, barrettes, or a band of paper stapled to fit children's heads
- a conical wizard's hat the students decorate themselves
- jewelry made with beads or noodles

Scenic Design

Allow the children to create immersive environments and set pieces to further engage with drama class. This can also help them further discover the setting of the world they are exploring in drama class as they engage in activities like these:

- draw environments with chalk outside, such as drawing railroad tracks and pretending to be trains
- create murals in the classroom using large sheets of butcher paper, such as a giant ocean scene followed by under-the-sea-themed drama games

- make buildings and other set pieces by painting large cardboard boxes for city-themed activities

- create giant flowers using long tubes of cardboard and paper and participate in drama games themed around a bug's-eye view

Examples of environments that children can create include the following:

- outer space
- a coral reef
- a fairy-tale kingdom
- a jungle
- ancient Egypt
- Santa's workshop

Props Construction

Allow children to create prop pieces that they might use during drama class, such as these:

- a knight's shield made of cardboard

- food

- wands

- any type of handheld item used in the drama, like a mirror or comb

See "Play Restaurant" on page 145 for a drama activity that involves the children creating props.

Masks

Create different masks that children can wear in the drama center or for an activity in drama class. There are a variety of ways you can create masks, from prefabricated masks that just need decorating to making your own using materials as simple as paper plates, baseball caps, cylinders of stapled paper, brown paper grocery sacks, and boxes. Your artists can make masks themed around whatever topic they are currently exploring, such as:

- fairy-tale characters

- rain forest animals

- savannah animals

- woodland creatures

- under the sea

- out of this world

- over the rainbow

- monsters

- ghosts and ghouls

Puppets

Puppets, created by students or provided by the teacher, can be incorporated into drama class in a variety of ways. The teacher can use the puppet to get the students' attention and have the puppet assist in giving the class directions. The puppet can also be a character in a dramatic activity, such as a teacher using a frog puppet to give the children a tour of a pond. The puppets can perform short skits about the day's theme, such as two puppets talking about going to the beach.

Students also enjoy playing with the puppets and creating their own stories, so include puppets as options in the drama center. Sometimes, students can express something using a puppet that they have difficulty expressing through their own bodies; there is safety in using a puppet to express themselves.

Various types of puppets can be created as an art component of a lesson and then incorporated into a drama play session, such as

- finger puppets

- hand puppets

- shadow puppets

Look at *A Show of Hands: Using Puppetry with Young Children* by Ingrid Crepeau and Ann Richards for more ideas to incorporate puppetry into your drama class.

Drama Inspired by Famous Paintings

You can create dramas based off famous works of art. Briefly discuss as a class what is happening in the paintings. What do the children see? What colors and shapes do they like in the painting? What questions do they have for the artist? How does the painting make them feel? Activities that can be done following the children's analysis and reflection of the paintings can be found at the end of the chapter.

Here is a list of paintings that can inspire dramatic activity:

Artworks of Animals:

- Bonheur, Rosa. *The Horse Fair*. 1852–1855. Oil on canvas. Metropolitan Museum of Art, New York.

- Hoji, Matsumoto. *Frog*. Eighteenth century. Ink on paper. The British Museum, London.

- Miskin. *Raven Addressing the Assembled Animals*. c. 1590–1620. Gouache on paper. The British Museum, London.

- Warhol, Andy. *Black Rhinoceros* from the *Endangered Species* portfolio. 1983. Silkscreen print. Private Collection.

Great Books Depicting How Artists See Animals:

- Blizzard, Gladys. *Come Look with Me: Animals in Art*. Watertown, MA: Charlesbridge, 2006.

- Carroll, Colleen. *How Artists See Animals: Mammal, Fish, Bird, Reptile*. New York: Abbeville Press, 1996.

- Micklethwait, Lucy. *Animals: A First Art Book*. London: Frances Lincoln, 2004.

  (*Animals: A First Art Book* is developmentally appropriate to read aloud, whereas the other two are useful only to share the visual references.)

Artworks of Cityscapes:

- Avercamp, Hendrick. *A Scene on the Ice Near a Town*. 1615. Oil on oak. The National Gallery, London.

- Bearden, Romare. *The Block*. 1971. Cut and pasted printed, colored, and metallic papers, photostats, graphite, ink marker, gouache, watercolor, and ink on Masonite. Metropolitan Museum of Art, New York.

- Caillebotte, Gustave. *Paris Street; Rainy Day*. 1877. Oil on canvas. Art Institute of Chicago, Chicago.

- Hiroshige, Andō. *Moonlit Street Scene in Edo*. 1856. Woodcut. University of Manchester, Manchester.

Artworks of Underwater Worlds:

- Calder, Alexander. *The Fish*. 1966. Metal, paint, wire, plastic, wood, glass, and ceramic. Hirshhorn Museum and Sculpture Garden, Smithsonian Institution, Washington, DC.

- Klee, Paul. *Magic Fish*. 1925. Oil and watercolor on canvas on panel. Philadelphia Museum of Art, Philadelphia.

Artworks of Gardens:

- Monet, Claude. *Bridge over a Pond of Water Lilies*. 1899. Oil on canvas. Metropolitan Museum of Art, New York.

- van Gogh, Vincent. *Field with Poppies*. 1890. Oil on canvas. Gemeentemuseum Den Haag, The Hague, Netherlands.

Artworks of Barnyards:

- Homer, Winslow. *The Milk Maid*. 1878. Watercolor over graphite on woven paper. National Gallery of Art, Washington, DC.

- Klimt, Gustov. *Garden Path with Chickens*. 1916. Oil on canvas. Destroyed by fire at Schloss Immendorf in 1945.

- Miró, Joan. *The Farm*. 1921–1922. Oil on canvas. National Gallery of Art, Washington, DC.

- van Gogh, Vincent. *The Reaper (after Millet)*. 1889. Oil on canvas. Van Gogh Museum, Amsterdam.

- Wood, Grant. *Spring in the Country*. 1941. Oil on canvas. Cedar Rapids Museum of Art, Cedar Rapids, IA.

Dramatic Activities Inspired by Visual Artwork

Body Building: Re-create a Painting!

Materials

- reproduction of a painting, still life, or portrait with several people

Act it out!

Allow children to re-create the paintings using their bodies:

1. Ask the class what they see in the painting. Perhaps the children notice inanimate objects, animals, or people in the paintings. Write a list of what students see in the painting.

2. Choose an area that will be used to reproduce the painting. Have the children sit in a line in front of the designated area so they can watch the painting being re-created.

3. Invite the students to create a still image together by adding each element of the painting, one person at a time. Let each person choose one aspect of the painting they will be re-creating with their bodies. For example, a child points to a tree in a painting, then goes and stands as a tree in the painting area. Let every artist become a different part of the painting.

4. Explain that you are going to enter into the painting. When you tap a child on the head, she is allowed to speak and answer a question as the object, animal, or person she portrays in the painting. Walk around the painting, tap a child on the head, and ask her a question, such as, "What is it like to be a tree?" or "What are you thinking right now, cow?"

5. Take a photo to let the class see how its re-creation of the painting looked.

Director's note

This activity could be used as a creative movement activity during drama class.

Spotlight on . . .
CREATIVITY &
THE ARTS

Materials

○ reproductions of landscapes or cityscapes

Act it out!

Have children perform a creative movement activity in which they are moving around in the different environments of the paintings:

1. Ask the students to look at the painting. Discuss what they see in the painting and how it makes them feel.

2. Instruct the class to line up; they can even hold hands if you're with a small group that would be comfortable with that. Tell them that you are all going to pretend to jump into the painting on the count of three. On the count of three, jump into the painting.

3. Once inside the painting, let the children decide the journey by asking them questions: "Where are we?" "What's it like here? Is it hot or cold?" "Who do we meet?" "What do we see?" Respond to what the children reply. For example, if a child says, "I see a pond!" you can say, "Let's go take a closer look at the pond! What do you see in and around the pond?"

4. When it's time to leave the painting, the class will line up again and jump out, back into the classroom.

5. Explore various environments such as Monet's garden or van Gogh's sunflower field. Fly through the night sky over New York City in Faith Ringgold's story quilt, *Tar Beach*. Swim underwater with the fish in Paul Klee's *Magic Fish*.

Director's note

This activity could be used as a creative movement activity during drama class.

Spotlight on . . .
CREATIVITY &
THE ARTS

Materials

o an image or a painting with people chatting or talking

Act it out!

Encourage the children to create dialogue for famous paintings:

1. Have the students sit where they can see the artwork. Give them an opportunity to look at the painting. Discuss the characters in the painting as a class: Who are these people? What are they doing? Why? What are the people thinking and feeling?

2. Finally, ask the children, "What would the characters say if they could speak?" Let the children share what their characters would be saying.

Encore!

Recommended artwork:

• the children in Winslow Homer's *Snap the Whip*
• the neighbors in Romare Bearden's *The Block*

How Does This Sound?

Materials

o a painting that contains something that could make sounds, such as animals, instruments, machines, or cars

Act it out!

Have children create soundscapes for famous paintings:

1. Look at the painting as a class. Ask the children, "What do you see in the painting?" "What sounds do you think are in the painting?"

2. Write down a list of sounds they came up with.

3. Go through the list of sounds and make the different sounds.

4. Put the sounds all together, having every student make a different sound of his choice.

Director's note

This activity could be used as a vocal warm-up activity in drama class.

Spotlight on . . .
CREATIVITY &
THE ARTS

Spotlight on . . .
CREATIVITY &
THE ARTS

Portrait

Materials

o reproductions of different portraits

Act it out!

1. Have the children examine various portraits.

2. Let students get into the same position as the person in a portrait.

3. Instruct children to create voices for each of the portraits.

Director's note

This activity could be used as an imaginative play activity in drama class.

Spotlight on . . .
CREATIVITY &
THE ARTS

A Magic Paintbrush

Materials

o *Animals: A First Art Book* by Lucy Micklethwait (optional)

o printouts of various artwork depicting animals

o a paintbrush

Act it out!

1. Look at how famous artists have depicted different animals, such as in *Animals: A First Art Book* by Lucy Micklethwait.

2. Tell the children you have a magic paintbrush. When you wave it, they will become the animal in the painting. When you wave it again, they must freeze.

3. Allow students to act out the different animals in the paintings, stopping and starting their movements using the paintbrush.

Director's note

This activity can be used as an imaginative play activity during drama class.

Spotlight on . . .
CREATIVITY &
THE ARTS

Materials

o examples of various portraits in which people are making different facial expressions

o *How Artists See Feelings* by Colleen Carroll

Act it out!

1. Look at a portrait or an image from *How Artists See Feelings*. Ask the children, "How does the person in this painting feel?"

2. Invite the children to re-create the facial expression. Ask them, "Can you make this face?"

Director's note

This activity could be used as an imaginative play activity in drama class.

○ ○ ○
Spotlight on . . .
CREATIVITY &
THE ARTS

Feel It Out!

Materials

o a work of art

Act it out!

1. This activity can be used as a reflection after looking at any artwork. Have the children look at the artwork.

2. Ask them to make a facial expression to show how the artwork made them feel.

Director's note

This activity could be used as an imaginative play activity during drama class.

○ ○ ○
Spotlight on . . .
COGNITIVE
DEVELOPMENT

SOCIAL & EMOTIONAL
LEARNING

Materials

o grocery store newspaper

o take-out menus

o paper

o glue sticks

o scissors

o plastic dishes and food

o small table and chairs

o apron/chef's hat (optional)

o costume box with various costume pieces (for restaurant goers)

Act it out!

1. Let the children create a restaurant menu by collaging food items from a grocery store newspaper. Discuss different kinds of foods. Encourage the class to create a healthy, balanced menu. What are different meals they could include in the menu (breakfast, lunch, dinner)? Let each student cut out food from the newspaper and collage it together into dishes on menu pages. Beneath the collage, you can write out what the meal is if the child wishes you to, or he can write something below the cutout images. Bring in some takeout menus so the class can look for ideas.

2. Let the children create a restaurant in the classroom. Arrange classroom tables and chairs to look more like a restaurant. Perhaps let the children make a restaurant sign. Add tablecloths, dishes, or floral arrangements. Put the menus the students created on the tables.

3. Ask the children, "Who would you see at a restaurant? Who works there? Who might go there?" Decide which different people will be at the restaurant. Who is the server? Who is the chef? Who are the diners?

4. If you have costume pieces, such as an apron, a chef's hat, or a hairnet for the chef, let the chef dress up. The server can also wear an apron and carry a small notepad and crayons to write down orders. You can also allow the restaurant goers to dress up however they would like. Perhaps they want to be themselves. Perhaps they want to be a tiger, firefighter, or fairy. If you have difficulty casting a role and no one wants to be chef, you can play the chef as a teacher-in-role. (You can also be a teacher-in-role as a restaurant goer, server, food critic, or busser.) If everyone wants to be the chef, then tell the actors that you can take turns playing the different roles, and then try to schedule a time to play the game again so children have time to play different roles. You

could also leave the menus in the drama center so the children can play restaurant during dramatic play.

5. Allow the group to play restaurant. The restaurant goers can enter the restaurant. The server can seat them, and the diners can look at the menu and order food. Have the server take their orders or pretend to. The restaurant goer will order something from the menu. The chef can pantomime preparing the food or can prepare the plastic food. A server can deliver the food. The diners can then pantomime eating the food. The children can even create fake money to pay for the food, if they want to. If there are any disagreements, try your best to help the children come up with a solution that meets everyone's needs.

6. Repeat the dramatic play again, if the children wish to, allowing everyone to switch roles.

Director's note

This activity could be used as an imaginative play activity during drama class.

Reflection Pictures
. . . .

Visual art can help children build upon the imagined world they discovered during dramatic play and drama class.

Materials

o crayons, oil pastels, or other drawing utensils

Act it out!

1. Allow children to draw pictures of what they saw or encountered during their dramatic play session.

   • If the students played a particular person or character, encourage them to draw that character.

   • Allow them to draw pictures of the various places they visited or things they experienced using their imaginations during drama class.

   • Students could also draw pictures about how they felt about today's drama class.

Director's note

This activity could be used as a reflection activity during drama class.

Visual art can help children build upon the imagined world they discovered during dramatic play and drama class.

Materials

o artwork that children created in art centers

o fancy dress-up clothes (optional)

o calm background music (optional)

Act it out!

1. Gather together the artwork children create in the art center throughout the week. You can also collect their work from over the last few weeks. While they are creating their art, ask them about their work, such as, "What is happening in your picture? Can you tell me more?"

2. Tell the students you are going to visit an art gallery. Ask them what an art gallery is. If they don't know, explain to them that an art gallery is a place that shares artists' work with others.

3. Tell them you are going to create an art gallery in the classroom by hanging all their work up for an exhibition.

4. Hang the students' artwork around the classroom or ask the students to help you decide where the work goes.

5. Place sticky notes about the artwork near each piece. These are the children's artist statements.

6. Let the students wear dress-up clothes for their art opening. Tell them that people get dressed up for gallery openings.

7. Play opening music. After everyone is dressed for the opening, walk around the classroom and visit everyone's work. Let each child explain their work to the class, or, if the artists prefer, you can read about the work from their artist statements.

Director's note

This activity could be used as a reflection activity after art center.

Spotlight on . . .
CREATIVITY &
THE ARTS

CHAPTER ELEVEN

....

Incorporating Literature:
The Storybook Drama

Bringing Together Drama and Literacy

Consider incorporating drama activities into story time or basing your drama lesson on a storybook. Bringing a picture book to life using dramatic techniques will help young children remember the story, as well as further connect with the emotional lives of the characters. Young children will reflect more on the setting of the book if they are creating sounds or acting out what the characters are doing. Instead of being passive listeners, children become active participants!

Using a storybook as the basis for a drama unit or drama class will give the children more insight into the world of drama class and help ignite their imaginations. Children will enjoy bringing their favorite characters to life and acting out dramatic moments. They will enjoy visiting the locations of their favorite stories. Choosing drama games based on storybooks will also give children an opportunity to further explore the characters and world of the storybook. This is also a great way for them to further reflect on the themes and characters in the storybook.

Dramatizing a Storybook in Class

Here are some ways you can incorporate drama into story time. Encouraging children to act out what they would see, smell, taste, touch, or hear in the book is a great way to teach them about the different senses. Don't forget to add in the corresponding parts of the body. What would the students see with their eyes? Smell with their noses? Hear with their ears? What would they taste with their tongues? What would they feel with their hands if they were doing what the characters in the book are doing? This will also help them be more invested in the story and become active participants, not passive observers. You can read the book once, then read again, stopping to do dramatic activities while you read.

Feel free to do several of these activities while reading the book. For example, children can pantomime actions with a prop and make a sound effect on the same page. Giving children something to do on each page keeps them active, attentive, and engaged as they listen to the story.

Director's note

It's really helpful to have a stand or easel to hold the picture book. That way, you will be able to move and act out moments in the story with the children. The children can also look at the picture to get ideas while you are not present. If you don't have a stand or an easel, don't be afraid to set the book down while you act something out with the class, or have another teacher perform the actions with the children. This allows someone to model the gesture or sound for the class and to act as a verbal and visual signal of when to start and stop the action.

Turn the Page
. . . .

Materials

○ This activity can be incorporated into any book or story.

Act it out!

1. Teach the children a waving gesture, such as moving your arms over your head. This means turn the page.

2. When it's time to turn a page, let the children use this waving gesture to signal turning the page.

Spotlight on . . .
PHYSICAL & MOTOR
DEVELOPMENT

Voicework
. . . .

Materials

○ This activity can be incorporated into any story or book.

○ The book used as an example is *Goldilocks and the Three Bears* retold by Jan Brett.

Act it out!

1. Let children recite the dialogue of different characters and explore making different voices for the characters in a book. For example, if you were reading the story of *Goldilocks and the Three Bears* retold by Jan Brett, invite the children to say the same line by each of the different characters. "Let's say the line, 'Who has been eating my porridge?' as a huge Papa Bear on the count of three. 1, 2, 3."

2. Encourage the class to say the same line as Baby Bear and Mama Bear as well.

Spotlight on . . .
CREATIVITY &
THE ARTS

Materials

o This activity can be incorporated into any story or book.

o The book used as an example is *Richard Scarry's Cars and Trucks and Things That Go* by Richard Scarry.

Act it out!

1. While you are reading the storybook, stop and ask the children to make various sound effects. For example, if you are looking at a busy street scene in *Richard Scarry's Cars and Trucks and Things That Go* by Richard Scarry, you can ask the children, "What do you see in the picture that makes a sound you can hear?" Cup your hand around your ear while waiting for their answers. A child might say, "A fire truck!"

2. Ask the children, "What sound does a fire truck make?" You can also point to different items in the storybook and ask the children, "What is this?" followed by, "What sound does this make?" Sounds children might be able to create include the following:

   • automobiles, planes, helicopters

   • instruments

   • animals

   • weather sounds (wind blowing, rain falling, thunder)

   • sound effects (running water, heavy footsteps, breaking a dish)

Spotlight on . . .
CREATIVITY &
THE ARTS

Do the Dialogue

Materials

o This activity can be incorporated into many different stories or books.

o The book used as an example is *Goodnight Moon* by Margaret Wise Brown.

Act it out!

1. Let the children repeat a short line or phrase from the book, using emotion. For example, if students are reading *Goodnight Moon* by Margaret Wise Brown, you can ask them to say, "Good night."

2. Then, when you are reading the book, give them a signal that it's time to say "good night" together, such as pointing at the class.

Spotlight on . . .
LANGUAGE &
LITERACY

CREATIVITY &
THE ARTS

Materials

○ This activity can be incorporated into many books.

○ The book used as an example is *I Am a Bunny* by Ole Risom.

Act it out!

1. Have the children look at an illustration carefully. Ask them, "What do you see?" For example, have them look at an illustration of a forest during the springtime, such as in *I Am a Bunny* by Ole Risom.

2. Ask the children, "What sounds might you hear in a forest?" Write down a list of things children say one might hear in a forest. For example, they might say, "Bees, birds, frogs, wind in the trees, and crickets." Let them look at the picture of the forest to get ideas.

3. Let children choose a sound they would like to make, or divide the class into a small number of groups, such as, "This side of the classroom is bees, and this side is frogs."

4. Like a conductor in an orchestra, when you point to a group and your hand is up, then the students in that group can start making their sound effect. When your hand goes down, they should be quiet. Practice a few times to give them the general idea.

5. To simplify this activity, let each child choose a sound that you would hear in the forest, and tell the group, "Together we are going to make the classroom sound like a forest on the count of three." Have a clear signal that communicates when it's time to stop, such as hitting a gong, making a gesture, or using a call-and-response phrase.

Encore!

See "Jungle Orchestra" on page 35.

Here are some settings that might be fun inspiration for children when creating a sound orchestra:

• a city

• a farm

• a jungle

• a rain forest

• an orchestra

Spotlight on . . .
CREATIVITY &
THE ARTS

Materials

○ You can incorporate this into many different stories or books.

○ The book used as an example is *Don't Let the Pigeon Drive the Bus!* by Mo Willems.

Act it out!

1. While you are reading the picture book, stop and ask the children how the main character might feel. For example, while reading *Don't Let the Pigeon Drive the Bus!* by Mo Willems, ask, "How is the pigeon feeling right now?" Let the children answer, for example, "Mad."

2. If you have time, you can even ask, "Have you ever felt that way? When?"

3. Then encourage the children to make a face that matches that feeling. For example, say, "Let's all make a mad face! On the count of three. 1, 2, 3, mad face!"

4. Let the children show you their mad faces. Do a mad face with the children. When you relax your face, they should relax theirs.

5. If you have time, you can even briefly discuss things you do when you are mad to make yourself feel better.

Encore!

Look at "Emotions Masks" found on page 53.

The following are storybooks that explore emotions:

• *Glad Monster, Sad Monster* by Ed Emberley and Anne Miranda
• *Wemberly Worried* by Kevin Henkes
• *The Color Monster: A Pop-Up Book of Feelings* by Anna Llenas
• *The Feelings Book* by Todd Parr
• *The Pigeon Has Feelings, Too!* by Mo Willems

Spotlight on . . .
CREATIVITY &
THE ARTS

SOCIAL & EMOTIONAL
LEARNING

Materials

- This activity can be incorporated into many different books or stories.
- The book used as an example is *Olivia Counts* by Ian Falconor.

Act it out!

1. Invite the children to act out what the characters are doing in a book, whether it is an activity, like dancing, or using an object, such as reading a book. For example, if you are reading *Olivia Counts* by Ian Falconor, Olivia might have three pots of paint and a paintbrush. Tell the children to imagine they are holding a paintbrush, like Olivia. Now they can dip their brushes in the paint. Ask them, "What color would your paint be? What are you painting?"

2. Pantomime painting with the students. When it's time to move on, say, "Now let's put down our paintbrushes and move on."

Smell That?!

Materials

- This activity can be incorporated into many different stories or books.
- The books used in this example are:
  - *Planting a Rainbow* by Lois Ehlert
  - *The Tiny Seed* by Eric Carle
  - *Gingerbread Baby* by Jan Brett
  - *I Am a Garbage Truck* by Ace Landers

Act it out!

1. If there is something particularly smelly in the book, you can stop to pretend to smell it. For example, if you are reading *Planting a Rainbow* by Lois Ehlert or *The Tiny Seed* by Eric Carle, you can stop to smell a flower. Have the children imagine that they are holding the flower. Have them breathe in deeply like they are smelling a flower. This can help them practice taking deep breaths. Ask the students how the flower smelled afterward. For another example, if you are reading *Gingerbread Baby* by Jan Brett, you can ask the children, "Can you smell the gingerbread cooking in the oven?" Take a moment to breathe in like you are smelling gingerbread. Ask the students to describe the smell afterward. Or if you are reading a book where the environment might have an unpleasant smell, such as *I Am a Garbage Truck* by Ace Landers, ask the class to smell the garbage truck. Then ask the class, "How does the garbage truck smell?" Have them make a face that shows how the garbage truck smells. You might need to hold your nose or wave your hand to diffuse the stench.

Spotlight on . . .
PHYSICAL & MOTOR
DEVELOPMENT

Spotlight on . . .
CREATIVITY &
THE ARTS

Materials

o This activity can be incorporated into many different stories or books.

o The books used as an example are:

• *Llama Llama Yum Yum Yum!* By Anna Dewdney

• *Eating the Alphabet* by Lois Ehlert

Act it out!

1. If a character eats something in the storybook you're reading, stop and pretend to eat the same item. For example, if you are reading *Llama Llama Yum Yum Yum!* by Anna Dewdney and the character is eating a peanut butter sandwich, say, "Pretend to eat a peanut butter sandwich on the count of three. 1, 2, 3." Pantomime picking up the sandwich, taking a big bite, chewing, and swallowing. Put the sandwich down. Wipe your mouth with a napkin if you need to. If time allows, you can even pretend to make a peanut butter sandwich by pantomiming the various steps.

2. Or if the book is about food, such as *Eating the Alphabet* by Lois Ehlert, ask the students to pretend to eat the item: "Can you pretend to eat a slice of watermelon on the count of three? 1, 2, 3." You can even pretend to hand out the watermelon to everyone.

Encore!

Consider looking at "A Sandwich" on page 67 for another great pantomime game.

Here are some different storybooks about food:

• *Cloudy With a Chance of Meatballs* by Judi Barrett

• *Pancakes, Pancakes!* by Eric Carle

• *The Very Hungry Caterpillar* by Eric Carle

• *Everybody Cooks Rice* by Norah Dooley

• *Monsters Don't Eat Broccoli* by Barbara Jean Hicks

• *How Do Dinosaurs Eat Their Food?* by Jan Yolen

Spotlight on . . .
CREATIVITY &
THE ARTS

156
. . . .

Chapter
Eleven

Get Ready . . . Set . . . Setting!
. . . .

Materials

○ This activity can be incorporated into many different stories or books.

○ The book used in this example is *The Snowy Day* by Ezra Jack Keats.

Act it out!

1. Have the children pretend to walk around in the environment of the book. For example, if you are reading *The Snowy Day* by Ezra Jack Keats, the class might take a walk through the snow. Have students imagine they are walking around the room through deep, crisp snow.

2. The children might even catch a snowflake on their tongues or make a snow sculpture together. Make sure they put on their mittens, scarves, hats, and coats before they go!

Spotlight on . . .
CREATIVITY &
THE ARTS

LANGUAGE &
LITERACY

Scene Study
. . . .

Materials

○ This activity would be a strong choice after many different stories or books.

○ The book used in this example is *Good Night, Gorilla* by Peggy Rathmann.

Act it out!

1. Let the children act out an important scene in a book. For example, if you are reading *Good Night, Gorilla* by Peggy Rathmann, let the children act out being the different animals sneaking behind the zookeeper. You can pretend to be the zookeeper or let the children take turns being the zookeeper, if they are enjoying the drama game.

Spotlight on . . .
CREATIVITY &
THE ARTS

LANGUAGE &
LITERACY

Materials

- This activity can be incorporated into many different stories or books.

- The book used as an example is *Where the Wild Things Are* by Maurice Sendak.

Act it out!

1. Create tableaus or still pictures of important moments in the story. For example, if you are reading *Where the Wild Things Are* by Maurice Sendak, you can have the children create a still image of the wild rumpus.

2. Have the children stand in a line. Tell the children, "On the count of three, we will make a pose of a wild thing during the wild rumpus, and we'll freeze like a statue. Here, I'll show you!" Demonstrate how to pose on the count of three as a wild thing statue.

3. Count to three and let everyone pose. Unfreeze to signify it's time to end posing.

4. You could also ask the children to pose while they remain seated. "Make your most fearsome wild thing faces and hold up your wild thing claws on the count of three. 1, 2, 3." Make a fearsome wild thing face and hold up your hands curled like claws along with the children.

Spotlight on . . .
CREATIVITY &
THE ARTS

LANGUAGE &
LITERACY

Using a Storybook in Drama Class

A storybook can be a great place to start when planning a drama lesson. A storybook can introduce the theme or topic of the day's drama lesson. Find a book themed around what the children have expressed interest in or what they are learning about in other subjects, such as science or art class. For example, if the children are learning about the ocean in science, then you can read them *I'm the Biggest Thing in the Ocean* by Kevin Sherry. You can do a variety of activities themed around the various animals and the environment of the ocean. You can also dramatize particular moments in the book or create a mural of the ocean to use as a set to create your own prequel or sequel to *I'm the Biggest Thing in the Ocean*. You could also create a short skit about some of the secondary characters in the book. Play the soundscape of a calming ocean during the cooldown and the reflection.

Here is a list of drama activities that are inspired from children's storybooks:

Literary Detectives

Materials

- a picture book children are not familiar with

- sticky notes

Act it out!

1. Cover the text of a picture book with sticky notes.

2. Show the children the picture book, and let them improvise the text for the book. Ask them, "What are the characters saying?" Write it onto the sticky notes. Do this for each page, as long as the children remain engaged. If they begin losing interest, only do it for a few pages. Make sure every child gets an opportunity to contribute if he would like to.

3. After you have finished, read aloud the book that the children wrote.

4. Remove the sticky notes.

5. Read the book again, this time without the sticky notes.

6. Discuss the differences and what the class liked about both versions.

Director's note

This activity is great for children to improvise dialogue and use critical thinking and creativity to decide what is happening in a picture book. This activity can be used as an imaginative play activity.

Spotlight on . . .
LANGUAGE &
LITERACY

CREATIVITY &
THE ARTS

Brown Bear, Brown Bear, What Do You See?

Act it out!

1. Have students stand in a circle.

2. The teacher and the children will say together, "Brown Bear, Brown Bear, what do you see?"

3. The first child will pretend to be a brown bear. Then she will come up with her own color and animal combination and say, "I see a [color, animal] looking at me." For example, "I see an orange ostrich looking at me."

4. The next child will then have to pretend to be an orange ostrich.

5. The teacher and the class will say, "Orange ostrich, orange ostrich, what do you see?"

6. The child playing the orange ostrich will then come up with his own color and animal combination, which the next child will have to pretend to be.

Spotlight on . . .
LANGUAGE &
LITERACY

APPROACHES TO
LEARNING

7. Play until you have gone around the whole circle or until children are emotionally ready to move on.

Encore!

You can also partner children in pairs, and they can play this game together.

This game is inspired by the beloved classic *Brown Bear, Brown Bear, What Do You See?* written by Bill Martin Jr. and illustrated by Eric Carle.

Director's note

This activity can be used as an energizing warm-up.

Becoming a Butterfly

Materials

o a calming woodland or meadow soundscape

o *A Very Hungry Caterpillar* by Eric Carle

Act it out!

1. Read *A Very Hungry Caterpillar* by Eric Carle with the class.

2. Have children inch around pretending to eat leaves like a caterpillar.

3. Tell the students to lie down and pretend to wrap themselves into their cocoons or chrysalises, safely hidden in some leaves.

4. Encourage children to close their eyes. Turn off the lights. Describe what is happening around them while they are undergoing their metamorphoses.

5. When they open their eyes and the light turns on, the students will break free from their cocoons and fly around as beautiful butterflies!

Director's note

This activity can be used as an imaginative play activity.

Spotlight on . . .
CREATIVITY &
THE ARTS

LANGUAGE &
LITERACY

This activity is also found in chapter 7, Creative Movement activities on page 88, but is adapted here for use after story time.

Materials

○ This activity can be used after reading many different books during story time.

○ The book used in this example is *Bee: A Peek-Through Picture Book* by Britta Teckentrup.

Act it out!

1. Read the children the storybook that will inspire this dramatic activity. Have all the children pretend to go to sleep when the lights are turned off.

2. Tell the students that as soon as the lights are turned on, they will wake up as different characters in the setting of the book. For example, "When the lights turn on, you will wake up as a busy bumblebee, flying around looking for pollen. You are surrounded by beautiful flowers. It's a beautiful spring day."

3. When you turn on the lights, the participants will wake up as the character you described. The children can move around the room. For example, they can move around as bees collecting pollen.

4. When it's time for the class to go to sleep again, turn off the lights. Remind the actors to pretend to go to sleep and close their eyes. Ask students who are lying too close to each other to move apart. Sometimes children may accidentally bump into each other, so it's important for them to have some space between themselves and their classmates.

5. When everyone is motionless and silent, describe the next creature or environment from the book that students will wake up as.

Encore!

The characters or environments you choose can be based on what the class is learning about that day. For example, if it's Halloween and you are reading the book *Five Little Pumpkins* by Dan Yaccarino, the group can wake up as:

• a bat

• a trick-or-treater

• a witch flying on a broomstick

• a mummy

• a werewolf

• a monster

• various jack-o'-lantern faces

Spotlight on . . .
PHYSICAL & MOTOR
DEVELOPMENT

Director's note

This activity can be used as a creative movement activity.

Act it out!

1. Have the children stand in a circle.

2. Tell a familiar story, such as Jack and the Beanstalk. Ask for volunteers to come to the center of the circle to act out different moments in the story for the class, or have the whole class perform different actions related to the story. At times, instruct students to create sound effects. You can direct actors to perform the following steps to act out the story:

- clutch your tummy like hungry Jack and his mother
- be the cow
- lead the reluctant cow to market
- take and count the beans from the mysterious stranger
- stomp like Jack's angry mother
- scold Jack
- throw the beans behind you
- start small on the ground and grow to become a huge beanstalk
- climb up the beanstalk
- get tired climbing the beanstalk—but keep going
- and going
- get to the top of the beanstalk
- look around in wonder
- be the goose that lays golden eggs
- say "Fee Fie Fo Fum!"
- walk like a giant
- squawk like the goose being kidnapped
- climb down the beanstalk
- dance with joy like Mother and Jack for having the goose
- climb up the beanstalk
- get tired climbing the beanstalk, but keep going

- and going
- get to the top
- look around in wonder
- play the magic harp
- sing like a magic harp
- say "Fee Fie Fo Fum!"
- walk like a giant
- climb down the beanstalk like Jack
- bellow "I'll get you!" like an angry giant
- climb down the beanstalk like a giant
- bellow at Jack like an angry giant
- climb down the beanstalk like a giant
- climb down the beanstalk like Jack
- chop down the beanstalk
- bellow like a falling giant
- fall down with a thud (Make a huge *thud* sound by sitting on the floor and stomping both your feet on the floor together. You may have to practice several times to stomp together to make a huge thud.)
- dance with joy like Mother and Jack for being rich

Director's note

This activity can be used as a creative movement activity.

Spotlight on . . .
CREATIVITY &
THE ARTS

PHYSICAL & MOTOR
DEVELOPMENT

Materials

o pictures of various baby animals hatching

o a picture book about animal eggs, such as these:

  • *Whose Egg?* by Lynette Evans

  • *What Will Hatch?* by Jennifer Ward

  • *Egg: Nature's Perfect Package* by Steve Jenkins and Robin Page

  • *Chickens Aren't the Only Ones* by Ruth Heller

Act it out!

1. Read the children a book about eggs, such as one listed above.

2. Have the children crouch like they are animals in an egg.

3. Show the class a picture of a baby dinosaur hatching from an egg. When you say, "Baby dinosaurs hatch," students will hatch from their eggs and roam around the room as baby dinosaurs.

4. When you say, "Return to the nest," the students will return to crouching as though they are a baby animal in an eggshell again.

5. Come up with a new animal for students to be when they hatch out of their shells, such as:

   • baby snakes

   • baby alligators

   • baby chickens

   • baby owls

   • baby fish

   • baby dragons

   • baby caterpillars

   • baby ostriches

   • baby squid

   • baby snails

   • baby sea turtles

Spotlight on . . .
CREATIVITY &
THE ARTS

APPROACHES TO
LEARNING

Director's note

This activity can be used as an imaginative play activity.

Materials

○ cardboard boxes big enough for a child to sit in, one for each child

○ book(s) about boxes, such as these:

  • *Not a Box* by Antoinette Portis

  • *Roxaboxen* by Alice McLerran

Act it out!

1. Read a book about boxes before doing the activity.

2. Give each child a cardboard box.

3. Tell the class that the cardboard boxes are different things. As a group, let everyone imagine their box is the different thing the class comes up with. For example, one child could say the box is a house. Have all the students pretend that their boxes are houses. When children seem emotionally ready to move on, have another child make a suggestion.

4. One by one, volunteers come up with ideas of what the box could be while the rest of the class pretends that the boxes are whatever the volunteer came up with. For example, if a child says the box is a sled, let the class imagine that their boxes are sleds racing down a snowy mountain. Ask the children to describe the experience of sledding. Where are they? How does it feel to be on the sled? You could also share ideas such as these:

  • a boat

  • a plane

  • a race car

  • a space rocket

  • a train

Director's note

This activity can be used as an imaginative play activity.

Spotlight on . . .
CREATIVITY &
THE ARTS

Hula-Hoop Homes

Materials

- Hula-Hoops, one for each child

- an age-appropriate book with characters that are animals in the forest, such as these:

  - *Because of an Acorn* by Lola M. Schaefer and Adam Schaefer
  - *The Busy Tree* by Jennifer Ward
  - *Lost in the Woods* by Carl R. Sams II and Jean Stoick
  - *I Am a Bunny* by Ole Risom

Act it out!

1. Read a book about animals in the forest.

2. Have the children discuss what kinds of animals live in the forest. Discuss where all the different animals live, such as these types of animal homes:

   - bears in caves
   - birds in nests
   - frogs in a pond
   - rabbits in burrows

3. Let each child decide what kind of animal she wants to be. Each child's Hula-Hoop will be her animal home.

4. Place Hula-Hoops on the floor, evenly spread out.

5. Tell the students to pretend to go to sleep in their Hula-Hoop homes.

6. Have the birds start tweeting to say, "It's time to get up," or you can whistle to signify that it's morning.

7. Tell the animals to wake up and go about their day inside their homes.

8. Then, instruct the actors to leave their homes and visit their neighbors in the forest. Perhaps the bear wants to take a swim in the pond with the frogs or eat berries with the birds.

9. After a long day, have all the animals return home to their Hula-Hoops and pretend to go to sleep.

Encore!

You can also complete this game with all the children being the same animal, and teach them individually about a day in the life of that animal, including what it does and eats.

Spotlight on . . .
CREATIVITY &
THE ARTS

APPROACHES TO
LEARNING

For example, a bear might do the following:

• catch fish in the river
• swim in the river
• eat berries
• climb a tree for honey
• get stung by bees
• get chased by bees
• scratch its back on a tree

You can even play the song "Bare Necessities" from Disney's *The Jungle Book*.

Director's note

This activity can be used as an imaginative play activity.

Wake Up, Little Chicks!

Materials

◦ Hula-Hoops, one for each child
◦ book(s) about baby chicks, such as these:
    • *This Little Chick* by John Lawrence
    • *Little Chick* by Lauren Thompson
    • *Flora and the Chicks: A Counting Book* by Molly Idle
    • *Busy Chickens* by John Schindel

Act it out!

1. Read a book about baby chicks.

2. Place Hula-Hoops, one for each child, throughout the space.

3. Have all the children lie curled up inside their Hula-Hoops.

4. Tell the class to imagine that the Hula-Hoops are nests and the students are baby chicks waiting to hatch.

5. Tell them to slowly stretch awake and break through their shells. Make your narration descriptive and from the perspective of a baby chick.

6. Then the children wobble on their new feet.

7. They cluck around the barnyard and greet each other.

8. After they have exhausted themselves, have them return to their nests and go to sleep.

Director's note

This activity can be used as an imaginative play activity.

Spotlight on . . .
CREATIVITY &
THE ARTS

SOCIAL & EMOTIONAL
LEARNING

Materials

○ soundscape of calming ocean waves or Saint-Saëns's "The Aquarium" from *The Carnival of the Animals*

○ a book about the ocean, such as these:

• *Sea Shapes* by Suse MacDonald

• *Mister Seahorse* by Eric Carle

• *The Rainbow Fish* by Marcus Pfister

• *A House for Hermit Crab* by Eric Carle

• *Swimmy* by Leo Lionni

• *Over in the Ocean: In a Coral Reef* by Marianne Berkes

• *Ten Little Fish* by Audrey Wood and Bruce Wood

• *Amos & Boris* by William Steig

• *I'm the Biggest Thing in the Ocean* by Kevin Sherry

• *A Swim Through the Sea* by Kristin Joy Pratt-Serafini

Act it out!

1. Read a book about underwater life. This allows students to see pictures of and learn more about the creatures they are going to pretend to be.

2. Tell your class that you will take a trip to the aquarium to see underwater life. Allow the children to freely walk around the space, imagining that they are visitors to the aquarium. Have them describe some of the ocean life they see. Play the music while they move around the space.

3. Provide a signal so the class knows when to freeze and when to move again. The signal can be turning the lights off, then on; stopping and starting the music; playing a noisemaker like a kazoo; or another way to get their attention. Have the children practice walking around the space a few times to make sure they understand the concept of freezing and then continuing.

4. Freeze the class. Tell the students that they will become the various creatures living in the aquarium. Describe each creature in detail: "Imagine that you are a crab. You are scuttling along the sand bed. You use your claws to wave to other crabs."

5. After each creature, freeze the children so they can hear the description of the next creature that they will pretend to be.

6. Let the students come up with ideas of what animals they can be. Some underwater creatures you may come across are:

- a crab
- a seal
- a fish
- a dolphin
- a sea turtle
- a squid
- a whale
- a shark

Director's notes

This activity can be used as an imaginative play activity.

Sound Effects Story
. . . .

Materials

o a picture book students are familiar with (optional)

Act it out!

1. Have students sit in a circle.

2. Tell the class a story, during which students can make sound effects. You can create the story as a class or read a familiar picture book. The story can be inspired by what children are learning about in class or by an issue or theme relevant to their daily lives, such as visiting the dentist for the first time or going to the grocery store to buy healthy food.

3. If you are creating the story as a class, consider making the students the main characters in the story. Ask them questions and take suggestions for what will happen in the story. For example, if the class is going to the zoo, ask them, "What animal do we visit next?" To involve children in the story, you can even say, "And then [child's name] said . . ." and allow that child to come up with her own dialogue. You can also ask the students what they would do next or what they saw, smelled, or heard in the story to let them have a part in creating the story you are telling.

Encore!

Here are some stories that lend themselves well to wacky and fun sound effects:

- walking through a haunted house
- a day at the farm
- a day at the zoo
- a day in a big city
- being in a boat during a storm

Consider using a storybook that contains a lot of potential sound effects, like the various zoo animals in *Zoo-Looking* by Mem Fox.

Spotlight on . . .
LANGUAGE &
LITERACY

You can also invent a story that contains a lot of sound effects, themed around what students are learning in class.

Director's notes

This is also a great activity to warm up the voice for drama class and engender young children to use their voices in expressive and creative ways.

I Think I Can!

Materials

○ sidewalk chalk and an outdoor area where children can use chalk

○ a book about trains, such as *The Little Engine That Could* by Watty Piper

Act it out!

1. Read a book about trains, such as *The Little Engine That Could* by Watty Piper, to the class.

2. Let children draw train tracks in the outdoor area.

3. The actors can pretend to be trains on the train tracks. They can take turns being the engine, who leads the rest of the class in a line along the tracks, or they can move around freely, exploring all the different train tracks.

Encore!

Let children paint cardboard boxes to look like train cars. Attach paper plates to the side with brads. Afterward, put the train cars on the tracks and encourage students to play with the train cars by themselves or as a group.

You can also create tracks indoors using masking tape if you don't have access to chalk or an outdoor space to create.

Director's note

This activity can be used as a creative movement activity.

Spotlight on . . .
CREATIVITY &
THE ARTS

Nursery Rhyme Activities

Classic nursery rhymes can be used to create imaginative drama sessions. Young children are already familiar with these characters and stories. They are also short and fun stories for young children to act out.

Change the Word!

Materials

o book of familiar nursery rhymes

Act it out!

1. Read a nursery rhyme that children are familiar with, but change one word in the nursery rhyme.

2. See if the children can guess which word you changed.

Director's note

This activity can be used to help everyone focus and center.

Spotlight on . . .
COGNITIVE
DEVELOPMENT

Hey Diddle Diddle

Act it out!

1. Recite the rhyme "Hey Diddle Diddle" as a class:

> Hey diddle diddle,
> the cat and the fiddle,
> the cow jumped over the moon.
> The little dog laughed,
> to see such sport,
> and the dish ran away with the spoon.

2. Cast different members of the class as different characters from the nursery rhyme.

3. Recite the rhyme again, and let the students take turns acting out the story as different characters.

Director's note

This activity can be used as an imaginative play activity.

Spotlight on . . .
SOCIAL & EMOTIONAL
LEARNING

LANGUAGE &
LITERACY

Materials

o Hula-Hoops

o cones

o masking tape

Act it out!

1. Sing the popular nursery rhyme "Mary Had a Little Lamb":

> Mary had a little lamb,
> little lamb, little lamb.
> Mary had a little lamb
> whose fleece was white as snow.
>
> And everywhere that Mary went,
> Mary went, Mary went,
> everywhere that Mary went
> the lamb was sure to go.

2. Create an obstacle course in the classroom using Hula-Hoops, cones, and masking tape. You can do this with the children or before class.

3. You are Mary and the students are lambs. The lambs have to follow Mary through the obstacle course to get safely home. Invent descriptions for the obstacles. Maybe the cones are a rocky mountain path. Perhaps the hoop is a tunnel. Perhaps there is masking tape on the floor as a road the lambs must cross (remember to stop and look both ways) or a river they have to swim across.

4. Get all the lambs safely home to their pen and celebrate with a dance party when you do.

Director's note

This activity can be used as an imaginative play activity.

Materials

○ a book (there are many different books you can use for this activity)

○ The books used as an example are *The Mitten* by Jan Brett, *10 Little Rubber Ducks* by Eric Carle, *We're Going on a Bear Hunt* by Michael Rosen, and *The Rainbow Fish* by Marcus Pfister.

Act it out!

1. Select a book with lots of characters, such as the different animals in *The Mitten* by Jan Brett, or a book about a group, such as the rubber ducks in *10 Little Rubber Ducks* by Eric Carle. Try to avoid books that have only a few main characters. You want the story to have lots of interesting characters for the children to pretend to be or a large group of the same type of character. For example, *We're Going on a Bear Hunt* by Michael Rosen is an excellent choice because it doesn't have specific characters and everyone can participate. If there are specific characters, allow the children to select which character they would like to play. For example, if you are dramatizing *The Rainbow Fish* by Marcus Pfister, let the students decide what kind of fish or other ocean animal they would like to be.

2. Act as the narrator reading the text. Tell the class to act out the play while you read the book.

3. If there are repetitive actions in a story, the class can come up with an action to perform. For example, you might read *We're Going on a Bear Hunt*, which is very repetitive. Come up with an action to do every time you say, "We're going on a bear hunt!"

4. If a character speaks, you can say the line first, then let the character repeat the line after you. For example, if you're reading *We're Going on a Bear Hunt*, say, "Oh no! We have to go through it!" then let the class repeat after you. If they know the story well enough, you can even say the line together.

5. Consider letting the kids improvise for a while. For example, if the characters are swimming through a river during *We're Going on a Bear Hunt*, let the class swim through the river.

6. Everyone takes a bow together at the end of dramatizing the storybook.

Encore!

• Consider improvising what happens after the end of the book. Perhaps the children can come up with a sequel or a new scene based off what they hypothesize will happen next.

Spotlight on . . .
LANGUAGE &
LITERACY

CREATIVITY &
THE ARTS

• During art class, let children create scenery, costume pieces, puppets, or props to use while dramatizing the storybook. Read the chapter on devising to get more ideas about improvising with pre-K students.

Director's notes

• Set up an audience of stuffed animals, puppets, and perhaps a fellow educator to watch the play.

• Create lines that all the children can say or perform together so everyone has an opportunity to speak.

• Play a soundscape of the environment of the storybook. For example, if the story takes place in a forest, play a woodland soundscape as background noise. You can also allow the children to create the soundscape of the environment at some point during the play.

• This activity can be used as an imaginative play activity during drama class.

PART FOUR

Bringing It All
Together

CHAPTER TWELVE

· ·

Devising Plays with Pre-K

What Is Devising?

A devised theatre performance is a play that is a creative collaboration developed entirely through improvisational acting. The children are the playwrights and the teacher is the editor and director, assisting the children in the creative process and bringing the work to the stage through editing and blocking. The process requires time, a rehearsal space, and an enthusiastic troupe of actors. Devising a production is best done with older, preschool-age students.

The process begins with researching the characters, themes, setting, and ideas being explored in the play. For example, if the devised play is about a day in the life of a bumblebee, the children would learn all about the lives of bees through watching videos, reading books, or looking at photographs and artwork of bumblebees, as part of the devising process. The children would also play imaginative drama games that would make them think about what it is like to be a bee. What would the average day in the life of a bee be like? What do bumblebees enjoy? What would irritate a bumblebee? What are bumblebees' aspirations and hopes? What is it like to live in a hive?

Actors also learn about the components of constructing a good story. During the devising process, and by researching the subject matter, actors will discover what stories they are interested in and how they collectively want to present their story.

Through improvising the various scenes and scenarios in their story, actors generate dialogue and flesh out the story they created. During this time, children can explore which characters they would like to be in the story. As the editor, you will help edit the script into the final version of the play and type up the script that will be used to block the final production.

After the actors have developed their script and you have typed up the final edited version, it is time to start rehearsing. Children will rehearse the play, as well as complete activities that help develop their characters and further explore the world of the play. Children can explore who their characters are and develop the physical and vocal attributes of their characters. For example, while rehearsing a play that takes place in the savannah with various grassland animals, students may explore manipulating their voices to sound like these characters, such as trumpeting like elephants or roaring like lions. They may also explore moving like these characters, such as galloping like gazelles or swinging their arm like they have an elephant trunk.

Children can also create various sets, props, and costume pieces. For example, if a play is set in outer space, the children might paint a huge mural of the solar system. If a play takes place in the ocean, they might make fish puppets. Children might make animal ears for a play that takes place in a zoo. There are myriad ways for children to create objects that can be used during the performance.

When the play has been rehearsed, it's time to culminate the devising process by sharing it with a supportive larger community. Theatre is meant to be shared and is an opportunity for connection between both artists and audience. Even if the performance is a casual one, children benefit from sharing the fruits of their labors.

The devising process ends with a final reflection, such as watching a recording of the production and discussing it the following day, and a celebration, such as a reception with loved ones.

Devising a play is an excellent way to culminate a drama unit. After children become familiar with drama class, devising a production is a way for children to utilize all their skills. It's a process that brings the class together and is worth exploring.

The Rewards of Devising

Devising plays with kids has a variety of rewards and benefits to young children developmentally, intellectually, and emotionally.

- This is an opportunity for students to create work as a community. Devising develops teamwork and a sense of camaraderie as everyone must rely on everyone else to make the production a reality. There are no small parts in theatre, only small actors!

- Children develop social and emotional skills as they shape the drama together. Children must respond to nonverbal cues of the other actors in the troupe. They develop empathy as they reflect on how their character is feeling at a particular moment in the play.

- Children must develop language and communication skills as they improvise. They must share their ideas with the community. They must discuss and reach a consensus on what they would like to have happen in their play. They must also come up with dialogue for the characters. Each actor should have the opportunity, if she wishes, to write a line of dialogue for her character to say!

- Devising promotes imagination and critical thinking as children decide on the challenge their characters will face and how they will overcome that challenge. The actors can imagine interesting characters and settings. They can also imagine various solutions and outcomes for the production. Children, while they are acting in the play, must imagine they are the character in that particular circumstance.

- Children have fun playing together in a way that is structured. Devising is an opportunity for children to explore and play together in a way that culminates in a shared experience that will include their whole community.

- Creating a class play can also integrate sets, scenery, costumes, and props that the children create in art class. Children will enjoy making pieces of visual art that will be utilized and shared with an audience in the final sharing of the production.

- Devising a play can culminate in a sharing of the work with loved ones, which gives children a sense of pride. Children appreciate the opportunity to have their hard work and creative fruits applauded and recognized by a supportive and loving community.

Crafting a Creative Collaboration

Devising a production has unique challenges but ample rewards. Children enjoy culminating their knowledge and experience in drama class to share with family and friends. You can use some of these techniques to devise a work during only one class period, or the play can be rehearsed several times and culminate in sharing a production with supportive loved ones. It's up to the community you facilitate and what you think would meet their needs. If you do intend to create a work to share with families and friends, make sure to schedule plenty of classes for the process. Plan for at least ten sessions. This really is about the children creating a world together, so give them ownership of the process.

Themes for Creative Collaborations

Choosing to devise a play themed around what the class is learning about in school, such as butterflies or life on a farm, will help children apply their knowledge and reinforce their absorption of the material. Here are some topics that children could further explore by devising a play:

- fairy tales
- outer space
- things that go beep (cars, trains, planes, boats, etc.)
- under the sea
- woodland creatures
- life on the pond

- on the farm
- a bug's tale
- animals on the plains of Africa
- animals in the jungle
- visiting a haunted house
- life in the Arctic

Children are very creative. Give them the space to explore and play, and they won't disappoint!

To Use or Not to Use?

Sometimes children want to reenact stories or pretend to be characters they have already seen in popular movies and television shows. You can choose to allow them to be these characters and reenact these stories, but you can also ask them to come up with something original that is similar to these characters and stories. This way, the actors will still have to use their imaginations to come up with the story, but they can be inspired by stories and characters they enjoy.

The setting of a play is where the play takes place. Perhaps it's a familiar setting, such as at school, on the playground, at the grocery store, or at home. Perhaps the setting is fantastical, like on the moon, in a candy land, or in a fairy-tale world. Perhaps it's a setting the children are learning about in school, such as in a beehive, on a coral reef, or on a farm.

Play several theatre games that take place in the play's environment to really immerse the actors in the world of the play. If the setting is the Arctic, go on an imaginary adventure through the ice. Or take the class on an imaginary guided tour of a coral reef, describing the environment in detail to the children as they sit silently.

Read books and do other activities that help the children become experts and learn more about the setting of the play. For example, watch a short film of life in a coral reef as a class. If the students are portraying insects, have them create a mural from an insect's point of view. Perhaps the children choose a familiar setting such as the school or local park. These types of settings are wonderful as well, since children can draw from their own life experiences when creating the work.

Creating a Character

Once the children have explored the setting of the play, they can create characters that would populate the setting. For example, if they are told the setting is in the woods, they might be squirrels, birds, or other woodland creatures.

Allow the children to create and decide upon the characters they will be playing. The children should create their own characters inspired by what they are learning about in class. For example, if they are learning about insects, allow them to decide on the insects they will be in the play. Some might want to be the same insect as someone else, whereas others might want to be something different. Maybe the children are different animals at the zoo, or they are all penguins living in the zoo's penguin house. The characters could be the inhabitants of a coral reef. Perhaps they are learning about animals living in the Arctic, and the children will choose to play different animals that make their homes there. You can have all the children play the same animal, such as butterflies or bumblebees, although they can each still have distinct personalities. This can be a great way to study or learn about a specific animal.

After children have decided on a character, allow them to draw a picture of their character. Drawing their character will give them the time and space to reflect on their character. What does their character look like? How would their character move? Where would their characters be (the setting for the play)? What does their character do? Additionally, drawing their character will help the children come up with potential costume ideas for their character.

Doing several theatre games such as "Character Freeze Dance!" (see below) that give the children an opportunity to pretend to be different characters will help them brainstorm and share ideas with the class. Creative movement games such as "Hula-Hoop Hike" (page 91), "Crossing to the Shapes" (page 94), and "Wake Up!" (page 88) will help children move like and develop the physical mannerisms of their characters.

Character Freeze Dance!

Materials

- music, could be culturally, stylistically, or emotionally related to the play the children are working on

Act it out!

1. Invite the children to move around the space and say hello to one another as their characters.

2. Tell the actors that they can move around the space as their characters when the music is playing. When the music stops, they must freeze. Turn on the music and let the children move around the space as their characters.

3. Stop the music. Everyone should freeze in place like a statue. You may want to practice a few times so the class gets the hang of the activity.

4. Then, instruct the actors to find another character to be their partner.

5. While still in character, the students ask their partners, "What is your favorite food?" Then their partners ask them the same question.

6. After the whole class has answered the question, turn on the music and let the students dance some more.

7. Continue playing for as long as you wish. Here is a list of questions the characters might ask one another:

   - What is your family like?
   - What do you like to do for fun?
   - Where do you live?
   - Can you show me a trick or something special you can do?

Starting from Characters instead of Setting

Deciding on the setting first can help children narrow down the characters they choose to play, but you can also allow the class to create the characters first, then decide where the story takes place.

One way to create characters is through costume pieces. Having costume pieces available for children to choose from can help them come up with fun characters.

A pink tutu and a gray baseball cap can inspire a child to play an ostrich. A green sequined skirt can become a mermaid tail. An old graduation gown can be a wizard's robe. Children will enjoy coming up with characters and being their own costume designers.

Sometimes, these characters might not normally populate the same setting. For example, a wizard, an ostrich, and a mermaid would typically be found in very different environments (a castle, grasslands, and under the sea). Let the children choose the setting for the play. Familiar settings the children know, such as a birthday party, grocery store, or playground, are all excellent choices because the children are already experts on these spaces and can imagine how their characters might behave in these spaces.

Once Upon a Time . . . Story Time!

Creating a story is fun but challenging. The children should be the creators, yet they need your guidance to create a compelling story. Remember that all stories need a beginning, a middle, and an end, and make sure that children have each of these components in their story.

The beginning should establish the world of the play. Every play's setting has its own society, code of morality, psychology, and aesthetic reality. The story should start off like a regular day. Ask the children what a regular day in the world of these characters looks like. What are these characters doing? For example, if the story is about bumblebees, then perhaps the story can begin with the bees buzzing around the hive.

You may need to implement a "one mic, one voice" rule, or provide a stuffed animal you pass around to whoever raised her hand, so only the person holding the stuffed animal can speak. You can explain, "All of you have important ideas. We want to be able to listen to your ideas. That's why we only speak one at a time, so we can listen carefully to each other. One mic, one voice."

Next, for the middle of the story, there should be a goal these characters have or a problem they must solve together. Ask the children what goal these characters could be working toward achieving. You may need to clarify what a goal is. You can also have the characters work together to solve a problem. Choose either a goal or a problem; the play only needs one or the other. Explain to the class the differences between a goal and a problem, or just ask the group to choose one or the other. For example, a goal might be the bees wanting to collect enough pollen to give as a birthday present to Queenie, the queen bee. A problem might be that a bear keeps stealing their honey, and the bees have to come up with a solution to scare the bear away for good to protect their hard-earned honey!

Next, discuss how these characters can work toward achieving their goal or solving their problem. Brainstorm as a class by asking children questions, such as, "What should the bees do to collect extra pollen?" "How can they solve this problem or achieve this goal?" "What would you do?" "How is it different than what the bee would do?" Perhaps the characters can try a few different approaches that don't work before solving their problem, although this is not necessary.

Finally, a well-written story needs closure, or an ending. Ask the children, "How does our story end?" For example, a child could say, "The bees work very hard and visit lots of flowers to get all the pollen!" Another student could suggest, "The bees decide to do a dance number instead for Queenie, who loves to dance!" Another child could say, "The bees help scare away a bear who is attacking their neighbor's hive, and their neighbor bees are so grateful that they help gather pollen to make lots of honey!" Write down and weigh equally all their ideas. "What do we think about the idea of the bees working extra hard to get all the honey?" Find something to celebrate about everyone's idea. "I appreciate how the bees are trying their best and working together to gather honey for their friend. They are very good friends." If time allows, encourage the class to improvise the various endings, acting out all or a few of the ideas to see which one the actors think is the strongest. Get a class consensus about which idea to use. Children can vote for the idea they enjoyed performing the best. Often, by acting out the various endings, students will discover which option they like the best. If you reach an impasse, draw straws so you remain impartial.

The story doesn't need to be too complicated, just include a strong introduction, a goal or problem, how the challenge is overcome, and the ending. Write down the narrator's lines that describe the main events of what will happen in the story. As the director, you or another teacher will be playing the narrator.

Here are examples of the narrator's lines in the play about bumblebees: "Once there were bumblebees who wanted to have a birthday party for the queen bee. They needed to collect lots of pollen to make honey. They worked very hard collecting honey, visiting many beautiful flowers. They had a wonderful birthday party for the queen bee and had lots of honey. The end."

This basic story outline will assist you in improvising scenes to begin developing dialogue. The outline helps communicate to actors what they will be doing in each scene and keeps them on track during the rehearsal process.

All for One! One for All!

Instead of centering your story on a main character, guide the troupe toward a story that utilizes all the characters. For example, a play about a bee looking for a friend would have a main character. A play about many bees with the shared goal of collecting extra pollen and hosting a surprise birthday party for the queen bee makes all the children the story's main characters and highlights the importance of working together to achieve big goals as a community.

A play that is centered on all the characters working toward a goal or solving a problem will include all the characters onstage, actively performing and engaged, for the duration of the play. This will be more fun for both the children and the audience. This also means the actors can do many of the activities together or as a group so that actors can choose between reciting their lines alone or saying them with the group, depending on their comfort level.

Improvise

Now that your class has created its story, start improvising the different parts of the story. *Improvise* means to generate dialogue by acting out the scenes. Improvise each section of the story one at a time. First improvise the beginning, then the section in which the characters face a goal or problem, the section in which they achieve their goal or overcome their challenge, and the ending. You should act as the narrator, explaining what happens and reading the main events of the story. The children get to invent the characters' dialogue and actions.

As the narrator sharing the story the class has already written, read aloud, "One morning, the bumblebees were buzzing and flying around their hive, working very hard to make honey." The children can then pretend to be bees flying around and working very hard to make honey. Ask the class, "Would any of you like to say a line of dialogue? What does your bee have to say? How is your bee feeling right now? What is he thinking? Remember, your line will be part of the play that we will share with our friends and family, so you will say it in front of others. You do not have to say a line unless you would like to." Sometimes many students want to say a line, and they must wait their turn while you write down their lines. Other times, none of them do. Either way is fine. Encouraging the children to say their lines together is a great option for classes with quieter students.

You can also record the improvisation session so you can type out the dialogue later rather than writing down dialogue as you go along. Don't add too many lines, and make sure most of the lines are ones the group can say together. Only give lines to the children who want to speak. It's fine for kids to change the wording of their lines during rehearsal and the performance as long as the idea is the same. If the actors change their lines too much, the next child to speak might become confused and miss his cue to act something out or to speak the next line.

During the initial improvisation when you are writing the script, notice any actions the characters do that the whole group can perform. If someone jumps when the characters are excited, then add to the narration, "Then the bumblebees jumped for joy!" Adding an action to the narration will give the students a cue to start doing that action.

Pen to Paper

Write out the final script, adding children's improvised sound effects, lines of dialogue, activities, and actions. Make sure your script isn't too long; for early childhood, keep the performances between five and twelve minutes. Each child's line should be only a few words or a sentence, depending on what is a good fit for her. Some children relish and enthusiastically memorize lines. Others find the idea of speaking in front of others terrifying and prefer to be part of a group. Let those who enjoy performing have the opportunity to speak alone and those who prefer the safety of a group to remain out of the spotlight.

When you have a final draft, read the script together as a class in a staged reading, before you start blocking (explained on page 217). Let the actors say their lines during the staged reading. Make any changes if necessary.

All Together!

Provide shared lines for the class to say together, such as, "The bumblebees grew excited and buzzed for joy." Then everyone can buzz for joy. This way, there is little stress about having to speak because everyone is speaking together; also, children who are too nervous to speak do not have to say the line but may join their peers if and when they feel ready. The children can play and improvise something a little different each time. For example, if the narrator says, "All the bees flew around the hive and went *buzz*," the children can perform this differently each time, flying in a different way and buzzing when they feel like it. The actors are still performing the same activity. They have space to explore and play while still keeping the same story; their blocking does not need to be the same each time nor does when and how they buzz.

The Role of the Narrator

Act as the narrator for the production. A good narrator is like a good accompanist to a solo musician. You are supporting the performers and guiding the story along. Provide the children with lots of descriptive action cues. For example, if you say, "The hungry caterpillars rubbed their tummies," the children will rub their tummies, whereas if you say, "The caterpillars were hungry," the children may not perform any actions.

As the narrator, you can whisper lines to children who may need extra help when it's time to say their lines. You can also say, "And then the elephant said, 'I heard you the first time!'" and let the child who is playing the elephant say the line afterward. Or you could give the child the cue, "And then the elephant said," and let the elephant finish the rest of the line.

If you are tech savvy, you can record the children narrating the story and create sound cues that let the children know what is happening next in the story, so they can act out the story accordingly.

Narrating the play live is a strong choice. Theatre is a live medium, about the ephemeral moment and special relationship between audience and performers. As the narrator, you become part of the play, which the kids appreciate. Additionally, this allows you to improvise, as the performance may be different from how you rehearsed. Sometimes actors make acting discoveries during performances, so having a flexible narrator can be helpful. Perhaps there is an actor who, when seeing the gathered audience just before the show is about to start, tells you that she has changed her mind about saying her lines and is too nervous to speak in front of so many people. As a flexible narrator, you can choose to skip her lines during the performance, give them to another character, or have the class say them together.

Face the Audience and Project That Voice!

Encourage proper positioning and diction, even for young actors. The audience will want to see the students during the production. When you are staging the play, remind the children to "cheat out," and face the audience even if they are talking to someone next to them. Also, engage the actors in plenty of vocal work to practice projecting their voices. Try putting a row of large stuffed animals at the back of the space and remind the children to project their voices so the stuffed animals can hear them. See the activity "Hello, Mrs. Elephant!" (page 38) and other activities in chapter 4 for ideas of how to help children develop and project their voices and speak clearly.

X Marks the Spot!

Blocking refers to the actions and staging that actors use in a performance. When creating the blocking for the production, make sure none of the children are obscured from view. Remind children that if they can't see the audience, the audience can't see them. Actors should always move to a place where they can see the audience.

Have easy-to-remember, uncomplicated blocking. A flock of penguins can waddle out in a straight line playing a game of follow the leader, which allows the audience to see each child. Having set pieces that kids can interact with will help their acting. For example, if they are bees, having large flowers drawn on murals on the walls will help the actors cross the space and gather pollen from the different flowers. Your narrating and giving clear directions about the actions on stage will help the actors considerably to remember blocking. For example, saying, "The kittens yawned, stretched out to the left, the right, the front, and curled into tiny balls before falling asleep" gives much clearer blocking than, "The kittens fell asleep." Remember, the more descriptive your narration, the more actions the children can interpret.

Consider putting a masking tape X or sticker on the ground so actors know where to stand on stage. This friendly reminder can help performers find the right place to stand and remember stage directions. You can even write the name or initials of the character or actor on the tape. You can also put a long line of masking tape on the floor of the performing space for children to stand on at the end of the production to do curtain call.

Stage Business

Stage business means the blocking or actions an actor does onstage. Making a sandwich, cleaning the floor, eating dinner . . . just like in real life, actors are always doing some kind of activity. It's important for actors to have stage business so they are not standing in a line reciting lines. In real life, human beings never stand around in perfectly straight lines, waiting to speak. Similarly, during the play, the children should always be doing something. For example, if they are penguins, maybe they are swimming. Maybe they are looking for fish. Maybe they are waddling around saying good morning to each other. Giving the students an activity to do and a clear goal will greatly immerse them in the world of the play and expand their acting choices. For example, if the children are bees at the queen's birthday party, maybe they are dancing with their friends. If they are gathering pollen, maybe they are flying around looking for pollen, trying to collect as much as they can in time for the queen's birthday party. It will get them moving around the stage with purpose and intention. They will be engaged during the entire rehearsal if their characters are constantly doing something.

Sometimes having props on stage can help actors. Adding a beach ball, pail, beach towel, and umbrella can really make them feel like they are at the beach. Be careful though: sometimes students will argue over props, so it can be helpful to discuss who is doing what with each prop before you start blocking the scene.

Also, don't be afraid to go propless and have students pantomime objects and activities. This is fun for children as well.

During the performance, you will be narrating these actions and activities. For example, the children pantomime making a sand castle during rehearsal. Record their devised activity, and then during the actual performance, say, "And then, the mermaids made a sand castle." The children will then know to pantomime building a sand castle. The quality of acting in the play will improve if you give students clear activities to perform in your narrated directions. The actors can concentrate on acting and not remembering what comes next in the play. They know that the narrator is there to move the story forward. They can enjoy acting and being in the present moment.

Practice Makes Less Scary

Rehearsing the play can help instill confidence in the young actors and make performing less scary. If possible, have the children rehearse in the space that they will be performing in. Sometimes, short rehearsals over a few sessions can be more productive than making the children perform the piece several times in a row during one session. Children can lose energy and focus during a long session. If you need to do a longer session, then make sure children get sufficient breaks where they can relax and do something unstructured. Even professional actors need a ten-to-fifteen-minute break every hour. It is physically, emotionally, and intellectually demanding to rehearse a play. Children are more productive and positive about the performance if they are allowed to take breaks. If you do take a break, play a drama game the children enjoy and complete a few focus and concentration activities to reenergize and refocus the actors before they jump back into rehearsal.

Having a small audience of one or two observers can make a huge difference to the actors' performance in a rehearsal. Consider putting out a row of stuffed animals to watch the rehearsal if you don't have an attentive audience member available to observe.

A Little Song and Dance!

Consider adding a little song or dance to the beginning or end of the performance. The children can create a short song or use a song they already know. For example, if they devised a play about animals having a tea party, sing "I'm a Little Teapot" at the end of the production. If the play takes place on Old MacDonald's farm, sing "Old MacDonald Had a Farm" at the start of the show.

You can also play some music and let the children choreograph a simple dance or perform a few simple actions. Feel free to join the performance and sing and dance with the children. They will appreciate your participation.

You can also ask the audience to join in. With the children, teach the audience the song and actions the children established, and then invite the audience to perform it together with the actors. The kids can feel connected to the audience and less shy if their friends and family are participating and having fun performing the song and actions as well. It's also fun for children to teach adults actions.

Set Crew!

Consider allowing the children to create a set for the production. The set can be as simple as a mural that they paint on a large roll of paper. For the play about bumblebees, the children could create giant flowers. Or maybe the play takes place in a forest, and the children can use sidewalk chalk to decorate an outdoor area to look like a beautiful forest floor. Maybe the play takes place in the actors' neighborhoods, so they paint various cardboard boxes to look like buildings. Children will be even more excited to share their work if they are also creating the set for the production.

Costume Creation

Allow children to create or find their own costumes. If they are portraying zoo animals, let the students cut out and decorate their animals' ears that you will glue to headbands or bands of paper stapled to fit the children's heads. Students can draw pictures of their characters that they can take home to help them find items they can bring to school for a costume. Let each child look through the classroom costume box to find something her character would wear. It will generate even more excitement for the final performance if the children are their own costume designers.

Rolling Camera!

Tell the children, "I will be recording the rehearsal today, so we can watch our rehearsal later." Sometimes students will take the rehearsal more seriously if they are being filmed. Share the recording of the rehearsal with the children so they can see themselves perform. Watch the performance as a class and briefly discuss the performance afterward so the children have an opportunity to congratulate each other on the strengths of the performance and identify areas for growth.

It's the Journey, Not the Destination

Be process oriented, not product oriented. Don't stress if someone doesn't feel like saying his line at the performance and you need to skip over the line. Maybe someone will miss an important cue during the performance, flying around to gather pollen before the narrator says to, while the other bees are still thinking about a good present for the queen bee. Someone else might have forgotten her wizard costume and had to borrow something from the class costume box, deciding to wear a firefighter's jacket when you would prefer she wear a sparkly, star-patterned cape that looks more like a wizard. Let her wear the firefighter's jacket she chose as her costume, not what you think looks more appropriate for her character. Maybe the ending the class comes up with doesn't make much sense (the bees decided to clean their rooms and the queen bee was very happy). The production is about the children, not winning a Tony. Don't worry if the cat costume the class created looks more like a zebra. Don't stress if a child misses a cue and starts singing the song intended as the finale in the middle of the production. Someone might say an unscripted line on the spot during the production, inspired from the moment. The show must go on, in theatre and in life! Often, these quirky moments are the ones the audience really appreciates and enjoys. Loved ones want to see their children having fun and being creative, not a perfect production. Enjoy the process and embrace the unexpected!

This is a wonderful opportunity for the students to play and create together. As long as they are having fun and have ownership over the process, the production is a success. Sometimes there will be disagreements, and negotiations will have to be made among the children. Your job is to act as a facilitator and mediator, not the main creative mind. Let them make as many of the choices as they can in the production.

Curtain Call

Curtain call is when actors come out after a performance and bow while the audience applauds. Practice the final bow at the end of the play. This is an important time for the children to receive praise for their hard work and to thank the audience for watching the production.

Reflection

Give the children space after the performance, perhaps waiting until the following day to discuss and reflect on their experience. What do the students think went well? What would they have done differently? Film the final performance so the children can see how they performed and celebrate their accomplishment.

Curtain Up!

If you want to share drama class with the troupe's fans but a performance isn't a good fit for your troupe, just invite loved ones to class and play the troupe's favorite games from drama class. Children often love to act with their families, and they are sure to have fun teaching loved ones their favorite drama games and acting together. There are plenty of ways to share the energy and values of drama class without the course culminating in a performance. Host a costume party where all the students can come as their favorite characters and can perform a short and silly skit together with their families for the rest of the class.

Example of a Twelve-Class Devising Schedule

Even though you are devising a production, start and end class with a greeting and saying good-bye ritual. Make sure to do warm-ups and a cooldown. It can be nice to incorporate books that are relevant to the theme of the production during the rehearsal process. This will help the children further immerse themselves in the world of the play. After rehearsing the production, play one or two creative movement games or other activities you know the children enjoy that are still related to the topic of the production. They may need to let loose after the considerable concentration and hard work that rehearsing a short play can require!

Session 1: Read a book about the theme. Explore setting by doing a few activities that take place in the environment of the play. Draw a mural for the set.

Session 2: Read another book about the theme. Learn about potential characters in a setting. Complete various drama activities centered around pretending to be different potential characters.

Session 3: Read another book about the theme. Create characters for the production. Draw pictures of characters and explore costume ideas with a costume box.

Session 4: Discuss the story. Decide on how the play starts, what challenge the characters face, how they solve the challenge, and a happy ending. Write out these main points as lines for the narrator. Explain to the children what a narrator is.

Session 5: Improvise the different sections of the play.

Session 6: Complete the first read-through. Always practice facing the audience.

Session 7: Block the show.

Session 8: Rehearse the show. Children practice projecting their voices.

Session 9: Rehearse the show. Learn a short song and dance.

Session 10: Rehearse the show. Find costumes.

Session 11: Dress rehearsal (in costume). Practice the curtain call.

Session 12: Perform the show. Celebrate with a brief cast and family dress-up and dance party, maybe followed with a healthy snack.

A Play by a Pre-K Drama Class

Cast of Characters

NARRATOR (played by teacher)

QUEENIE BEE (played by another teacher using sock puppet)

BEES

BEES WHO WANTED LINES:

AHMED THE BEE

CARLOS THE BEE

ISABEL THE BEE

SASHA THE BEE

MIHYE THE BEE

SHATOYA THE BEE

Setting

Inside the hive

A beautiful meadow

Set

Various oversize flowers, made with wrapping paper rolls painted green for the
stem and tissue paper for blossoms, around the edges of the stage area

A mural painted to look like the inside of the hive, created using hexagon sponges
stamped on the paper with yellow and red paint, as well as gold glitter paint

Costumes

Yellow and black clothing. Some children painted stripes on their clothes.

Pipe cleaners wrapped around headbands to make antennae. Some children added
foam shapes to the ends of the antennae.

Wings made from floral-patterned bedsheets, cut as triangles the length of the
students' arms. Wings are secured to children's wrists with elastic hairbands and
are safety pinned from the center of triangle to the neck of each child's T-shirt.

Props

Bee sock puppet made by child to be Queenie the queen bee

Sounds

"Flight of the Bumblebee" by Nikolai Rimsky-Korsakov

Upbeat dance music

Smartphone or computer, with optional speaker, to play sound cues

NARRATOR   One morning, the bumblebees were buzzing and flying around their hive working very hard to make honey.

(Play song "Flight of the Bumblebee" by Rimsky-Korsakov. BEES fly around, buzzing loudly. Turn off music before BEES speak.)

NARRATOR   All the bees buzzed.

ALL THE BEES   Buzzzzz.

NARRATOR   Ahmed the Bee said, "We live in a hive."

AHMED THE BEE   We live in a hive.

NARRATOR   "I work very hard," said Carlos the Bee.

CARLOS THE BEE   I work very hard.

NARRATOR   Isabel the bee said, "Me too!"

ISABEL THE BEE   Me too!

NARRATOR   Then Queenie the queen bee entered the hive.

(QUEENIE BEE enters the hive.)

All the bees bowed and curtsied for the queen.

(BEES bow and curtsy for QUEENIE BEE.)

Queenie said, "Thank you! It's my birthday tomorrow! Hooray!"

QUEENIE BEE   Thank you! It's my birthday tomorrow! Hooray!

NARRATOR   Then she left. All the bees waved and said, "Good-bye, Queenie!"

(BEES wave bye-bye.)

ALL THE BEES   Good-bye, Queenie!

NARRATOR   Sasha the Bee said, "Queenie's birthday is tomorrow?!"

SASHA THE BEE   Queenie's birthday is tomorrow?!

NARRATOR   The bees buzzed around nervously and discussed what to do.

(BEES buzz nervously and whisper to each other.)

The bees decided to work extra hard gathering pollen to make honey. The bees flew out of the hive to collect pollen from all the flowers to make honey.

(Play "Flight of the Bumblebee" again. BEES fly around to all the flowers on the edge of the stage and pantomime bringing pollen back to the hive area.)

NARRATOR	The bees collected a lot of pollen. They made a lot of honey for Queenie's birthday! They jumped for joy!
	(BEES jump for joy!)
	Mihye the Bee said, "We did it!"
MIHYE THE BEE	We did it!
NARRATOR	Shatoya the Bee said, "Yay!"
SHATOYA THE BEE	Yay!
NARRATOR	Queenie entered the hive.
	(QUEENIE BEE enters.)
	Queenie gasped at the sight of all the honey!
	(QUEENIE BEE gasps.)
	All the bees said, "Surprise!"
ALL THE BEES	Surprise!
NARRATOR	"Thank you!" Queenie said.
QUEENIE BEE	Thank you!
NARRATOR	Queenie went on to say, "This is the best birthday ever and you are my best friends!"
QUEENIE BEE	This is the best birthday ever and you are my best friends!
NARRATOR	The bees came and hugged Queenie.
	(BEES come and hug QUEENIE BEE.)
	All the bees said, "Happy birthday, Queenie!"
ALL THE BEES	Happy birthday, Queenie!
NARRATOR	The bees then danced the night away!
	(Play upbeat music. BEES perform dance.)
	Now it's your turn to learn the Bee Dance! Everyone stand up.
	(Let children teach audience the Bee Dance. Perform the dance together!)
	The end! Let's all line up and take a bow together!
	(CAST takes a final bow together. Audience applauds.)

THE END

Appendix

The Seasons: Four Sample Lesson Plans

SPRING
. . . .

Date: August 12, 2017   By: Lavinia Roberts

Theme/Learning Goals:

The children will learn about the season of spring. What is the weather like? What do
    animals and people do during the spring?

Materials:

a woodland soundscape, birds chirping, or perhaps Antonio Vivaldi's "Spring" from *The
    Four Seasons*

A Very Hungry Caterpillar by Eric Carle

"Waltz of the Flowers" from *The Nutcracker* by Pyotr Tchaikovsky

colorful ribbons or scarves (optional)

Opening Circle and Breathing Activity (2–3 minutes)

Butterfly Breath (1 minute or less) (This activity can be found on page 25.)

When inhaling through your mouth, raise your arms over your head, like gentle
    butterfly wings.

When exhaling, float your wings back down.

Bumblebee Breath (1 minute or less) (This activity can be found on page 25.)

Breathe in through your nose.

Exhale through the mouth, making a faint humming sound.

Vocal Warm-up (4–5 minutes)

Spring Rains Are Falling Down (2–3 minutes)

Sing to the tune of "London Bridge Is Falling Down":

Spring rains are falling down,

falling down, falling down.

Spring rains are falling down,

welcome spring.

Create a Rainstorm (2 minutes or less) (This activity can be found on page 35.)

Start by blowing through your teeth, making the sound of the wind.

Snap your fingers; the rain is starting!

Pound on your lap; the rain is falling harder!

Pound on the floor with your feet and make the sound of thunder with your voices. It's become a thunderstorm!

Pound on your lap; the rainstorm is getting lighter.

Snap your fingers; the rainstorm is lessening.

Whistle or cheep like birds chirping; the storm is finally over!

Concentration, Focus, and Listening Warm-up (1–2 minutes)

Circle Stretch (See the full activity on page 40.)

Have the class stand in a circle with their arms extended, fingers touching their neighbors'.

Energizing Body Warm-up (5 minutes)

Across the Classroom (See the full activity on page 55.)

Materials: a woodland soundscape, birds chirping, or perhaps Antonio Vivaldi's "Spring" from *The Four Seasons*

Line up the children along a wall, not in front of each other but spread out evenly along the wall.

Instruct the students in how to cross the classroom using different movements. Turn on the music to help create a fun and engaging environment.

Once the children reach the wall on the other side, they should wait for instructions about the next movement they will use to cross the classroom. Allow students to offer suggestions. Here are ideas for different movements the class could perform to cross the room: as baby bunnies   as ducks   as butterflies   as bumblebees

as though they are caught in a spring rain shower—umbrellas out

as if they are playing in the rain

as though they are skipping in a beautiful field of flowers

as though they are robins, singing joyfully

Imaginative Play Activity (8–10 minutes)

Becoming a Butterfly (This activity can be found on page 159.)

Materials: a calming woodland or meadow soundscape, *A Very Hungry Caterpillar* by Eric Carle

Read *A Very Hungry Caterpillar* by Eric Carle.

Have children inch around pretending to eat leaves like a caterpillar.

Tell the students to lie down and pretend to wrap themselves into their cocoons or chrysalises, safely hidden in some leaves.

Encourage children to close their eyes. Turn off the lights. Describe what is happening
around them while they are undergoing their metamorphoses.

When they open their eyes and the light turns on, the students will break free from
their cocoons and fly around as beautiful butterflies!

Creative Movement Activity (8–10 minutes)

Flower Power (3–5 minutes) (This activity can be found on page 129.)

Materials: "Waltz of the Flowers" from *The Nutcracker* by Pyotr Tchaikovsky, colorful
ribbons or scarves (optional)

Explain to the children that this piece of music is titled "Waltz of the Flowers." Have
them close their eyes and imagine what type of flower they will be. Ask each child if
he wants to share what kind of flower he is. The students who want to share can tell
the class what kind of flower they are. Tell them that when the music starts, they can
move around the space as though they are flowers in the garden.

Play the music. Allow the children to move around the space imagining that they are
flowers in a garden. If available, give students the option to dance with colorful
scarves or with ribbons tied to elastic bands.

(If the children are engaged with the first movement activity, continue. If the children
are emotionally ready to move on, complete the "Busy Bees" activity below to use the
full ten minutes.)

Busy Bees (3–5 minutes) (This activity can be found on page 129.)

Materials: "Flight of the Bumblebee" from *The Tale of Tsar Saltan* by Nikolai Rimsky-
Korsakov

Tell the children that this piece of music was inspired by bumblebees.

While they are still sitting, have the students buzz like angry bees, followed by sad bees,
then happy bees. Listen to the music. Ask the children how they think the bee in the
music feels.

Explain to them that when the music starts, they can move like busy bees. When the
music stops, tell them to freeze.

Play the music again. Allow the children to be bumblebees, flying around the classroom,
collecting nectar to make honey.

Cooldown (5 minutes)

Yoga Poses (2 minutes) (Find more yoga poses on pages 44–45.)

Guide the children through the following yoga poses:

Tree Pose (1 minute or less)

Plant your feet firmly into the earth. Raise one foot, placing it firmly on your other

thigh as high as you can. Place your hands together high over your head or at your

chest.

Mountain Pose (1 minute or less)

Your feet are firmly planted on the ground, your spine is long and aligned, your shoul-

ders are rolled back, and your palms are pressed together as you take deep breaths.

A Spring Day Cooldown (2–3 minutes)

Have the children sit in a circle.

Tell them to imagine they are planting a seed in the ground in front of them.

Have them bring their fingers down like spring rain onto their garden.

Students turn their arms into a circle, like the sun overhead, to warm their garden.

They turn their hands into birds, flying over their garden.

They make their fingers into flowers growing up from the ground.

The students breathe in deeply to smell all the beautiful flowers they have planted in

their garden.

Closing Circle and Reflection (2–3 minutes)

Closing Circle Time (This activity can be found on page 107.)

Class begins and ends with students seated or standing in a circle, facing each other.

Here is a list of questions you could ask students during a closing circle time:

What did you enjoy about drama today?

What would you like to learn more about?

Closing Ritual (2–3 minutes)

Encore! Take a Bow (This activity can be found on page 109.)

Have all the students stand in a circle.

Each child bows, one at a time, while the others applaud her.

Take a final bow together as a class.

Give each other a final round of applause by clapping hands while moving them in

a circle.

Art Component:

Create giant flowers using old wrapping paper cardboard rolls or rolled-up green paper,

and then sponge paint onto paper or add tissue paper to create the blooms. You can

also use these giant flowers as the set for children to visit when they are bees or but-

terflies searching for nectar.

SUMMER
. . . .

Date: August 12, 2017   By: Lavinia Roberts

Theme/Learning Goals: Children will learn about the season of summer and about visiting the beach. What is the weather like? What do people do during the summer? What is it like to visit the beach? What do you do there?

Materials:

pinwheels, one for each child

Hula-Hoops

ocean soundscape

Opening Circle and Breathing Activity (3–5 minutes)

Pinwheel Breath (See the full activity on page 28.)

Materials: pinwheels, one for each student

Have students sit in a circle.

Practice taking a few deep, diaphragmatic breaths with the children, where their tummies expand when they inhale and go in when they exhale. Have them place their hands on their tummies so they can feel the air coming in and expanding their diaphragm when they inhale and go out when they exhale.

Give each student a pinwheel.

Have the class practice taking long breaths in and out. When the children exhale, they should breathe out onto the pinwheel, making it spin.

Allow students to see how long they can exhale. Have them try to exhale longer each time. See if they can exhale for two seconds, then three seconds, then four seconds, then five seconds. Count using your fingers held up in the air so children can see how many seconds they have spent exhaling.

Vocal Warm-up (5–8 minutes)

Summer Sun Is Shining Down (2–3 minutes)

Sing to the tune of "London Bridge Is Falling Down":

Summer sun is shining down,

shining down, shining down.

Summer sun is shining down,

welcome summer.

Concentration, Focus, and Listening Warm-up (3–5 minutes)

On the Beach! In the Ocean! (This activity can be found on page 41.)

Have the children stand in a line side by side.

Tell them to close their eyes and imagine they are on the shore of the beach. The waves of the ocean are in front of them.

Instruct children to open their eyes. When you say "in the ocean," the children jump forward one hop like they are jumping into the waves. When you say "on the beach," they jump backward one hop.

Say "on the beach" and "in the ocean" at various speeds. Sometimes say "on the beach" or "in the ocean" twice in a row to make sure the students are listening.

Congratulate the children for being good listeners.

Energizing Body Warm-up (3–5 minutes)

Good Morning! Let's . . . (See the full activity on page 51.)

Have children stand in a circle.

Say "Good morning! Let's . . ." and then pantomime an activity you might do in the morning as a class, such as stretch awake.

Go to the next person and have him say, "Good morning! Let's . . ." and pantomime stretching awake, and then add a new activity, such as brushing his teeth.

Go around the circle, adding something new each time. You can do all the previous activities each time or just the new activity, depending on the group's size and abilities.

Imaginative Play Activity (8–10 minutes)

Day at the Beach (See the full activity on page 72.)

Have the children sit in a circle.

Tell the students a story about a day at the beach. Allow them to create sound effects and pantomime various parts of the story.

Creative Movement Activities (8–12 minutes)

Hula-Hoop Hike (8–10 minutes) (This is a variation of the activity on page 91.)

Materials: fun music (perhaps silly surfer rock like The Beach Boys) or an ocean soundscape; Hula-Hoops; photographs of the various animals children might see at the beach or in the ocean (optional, if you don't think the students are familiar with them); *Fish Magic* by Paul Klee, to give children an idea of an underwater world

Place Hula-Hoops around the classroom or yard, one for each student.

Give participants instructions to move to different Hula-Hoops. There can only be one
child per Hula-Hoop. When you tell the students to cross to a new Hula-Hoop, give
them clear instructions for how they are to do so. Possibilities for movements
include the following:

Swim to another Hula-Hoop as a fish.

Swim to another Hula-Hoop as a scuba diver.

Skuttle to another Hula-Hoop as a crab.

Walk to another Hula-Hoop like you are eating an ice cream cone.

Wiggle your arms and legs to another Hula-Hoop like you are an octopus.

Swim to another Hula-Hoop like a great white shark.

Fly to another Hula-Hoop like a seagull.

Surf to another Hula-Hoop on your surfboard.

(If the children are engaged with the first movement activity, continue. If they are emotionally ready to move on, do the "Freeze Dance" activity to use the full ten minutes.)

Freeze Dance (3–5 minutes)

Materials: soundscape of ocean waves or underwater-themed music, such as "Under
the Sea" from Disney's *The Little Mermaid*; masking tape to divide the room in half

Begin by playing music for this classic movement game.

While the music is playing, children dance.

When the music stops, children have to freeze.

If students continue moving when the music stops, they cross to the other side of the
room. The children who are on the opposite side of the room can move when the
music stops, while the other children dance when the music is playing.

Cooldown (3–5 minutes)

Yoga Under the Sea (See more yoga poses on page 45.)

Lie on the ground on your tummy and bring your arms up in front of you like a diver.
Lift your feet up, diving into the ocean (superhuman yoga pose).

Now flap your arms and tail (feet), becoming a dolphin swimming in the ocean (dolphin
yoga pose).

Now, with your legs straight out behind you, arch your back so your chest is directed
upward. Bring your flippers (arms) together like a seal (seal yoga pose).

Then, lie on your back. Move your arms and legs as though you are doing a backstroke
in place (swimmer stretch).

Now, become a starfish. Stretch your arms and legs apart as wide as you can (starfish
stretch).

Breathe in through your nose, then breathe out like you are blowing giant bubbles under the sea.

Closing Circle and Reflection (3–5 minutes)

Breaking News! (This activity can be found on page 107.)

As teacher-in-role, pretend to be a news reporter, reporting live from your preschool or child care center.

Interview each child about how she felt about the day's drama class, as though you are reporting the news on TV. What did the children enjoy? What was their favorite part of class?

Closing Ritual (3–5 minutes)

Encore! Take a Bow (This activity can be found on page 109.)

Have all the students stand in a circle.

Each child bows, one at a time, while the others applaud him.

Take a final bow together as a class.

Give each other a final round of applause by clapping hands while moving them in a circle.

Art Component:

Materials:

oil pastels or crayons

watercolors

paintbrushes

cups for water

paper

Music: "The Aquarium" from *The Carnival of the Animals* by Camille Saint-Saëns, *Water Music* by George Frideric Handel.

Famous artwork: *Fish Magic* by Paul Klee

Create a giant mural of the ocean to use as a set piece or as a way for the students to reflect on their underwater adventure. You can also have the students draw the various sea life using oil pastels or crayons. Have them paint the water using watercolor paints. The oil pastels are water resistant and won't absorb any of the paint, leaving the original image visible. Play classical music inspired by the ocean while the children work, such as "The Aquarium" by Camille Saint-Saëns, and consider looking at and briefly discussing *Fish Magic* by artist Paul Klee.

FALL
. . . .

Date: August 12, 2017   By: Lavinia Roberts

Theme/Learning Goals:

Children will learn about the season of fall. What is the weather like during fall? What

 do people wear and do during the season of fall?

Materials:

colored scarves, if possible the colors of autumn leaves

Breathing/Circle Activity (2–3 minutes)

Wind in the Trees (1 minute or less) (This activity can be found on page 24.)

Have students breathe in deeply through their noses.

Then students release their breath through their mouths and their teeth to make a

 noise like wind in the trees when they exhale.

The children can even wave their arms, with fingers extended like tree branches in the

 wind.

Leaves Falling (1 minute or less) (This activity is a variation of "Butterfly Breath" found on page 25.)

Have students inhale deeply, lifting their arms up like tree branches.

When they breathe out, they let their arms fall like gently falling leaves.

Vocal Warm-up (3–5 minutes)

Autumn Leaves Are Falling Down

Materials: red, yellow, and/or orange scarves (optional)

Sing to the tune of "London Bridge Is Falling Down":

Autumn leaves are falling down,

falling down, falling down.

Autumn leaves are falling down,

welcome fall.

Children can move their fingers like leaves, or they can wave scarves if you have them.

Concentration, Focus, or Listening Warm-up (3–5 minutes)

Big Tree! Little Tree! (This activity can be found on page 40.)

Have children stand in a circle.

Demonstrate the actions for big tree and little tree for the children. When you say "big tree," spread your body out as tall and big as you can. When you say "little tree," make your body as small as you can. Perform the actions together as a group. Say "big tree" and "little tree" together as a class.

Go around the circle. One child will say "big tree" while completing the action, then the next child will say "little tree" while doing the action.

Energizing Body Warm-up (8–10 minutes)

Jack-O'-Lantern Faces (3–5 minutes) (This is a variation of "Emotions Masks" on page 53.)
Ask the actors to stand in a circle facing each other.

Tell the children you are going to spin around, and when you are facing the front again, you will have a face like a happy jack-o'-lantern. Demonstrate for them how to spin around and "put on" a face like a happy jack-o'-lantern. Encourage them to engage and stretch out their face muscles.

Tell the children, "We are going to spin around on the count of three and put on a sad jack-o'-lantern face. 1, 2, 3!" Everyone should spin around wearing their best sad jack-o'-lantern face.

Here are some other kinds of jack-o'-lantern faces you can make:

angry   scared   surprised

Across the Classroom (5–7 minutes) (This activity can be found on page 55.)
Materials: music (recommended)

Clear the classroom space or play outside in an open area. Line up the children along a wall, not in front of each other but spread out evenly along the wall.

Instruct the students in how to cross the classroom using different movements. Turn on the music to help create a fun and engaging environment.

Once the children reach the wall on the other side, they should wait for instructions about the next type of movement they will use to cross the classroom.

Allow students to offer suggestions for different movements. Here are ideas for different movements the class could perform to cross the room:

as though they are leaves blowing in the wind

as though they are raking leaves

as though they are jumping through tall piles of leaves

as though they are carrying a heavy pumpkin

as though they are migrating geese, flying long distances

Imaginative Play Activity (8–10 minutes)

Follow the Flock (This activity can be found on page 69.)

Discuss why and how birds migrate. By flying in a V formation, birds carefully position their wingtips and synchronize their flapping to catch the preceding bird's updraft—and save energy during their long flight.

As the teacher, you will be the leader, leading the flock. The children, or other birds, will get behind you in a V shape. Like follow the leader, the other birds will try to follow your movements exactly as you move around the space.

Create a story, as a class, of the adventure you go on as a flock of birds.

Ask your class various questions about what is happening during your migration so you are creating the story together. "What might our flock see flying through the air? What will we fly over during our adventure? What will the weather be like? Will the air be warm or cold? How do we feel right now? Are we excited, scared, or tired?" Think about all these elements as you fly your flock through the sky.

Creative Movement Activities (7–9 minutes)

Walk the Line (This activity can be found on page 94.)

Materials: "Fall" from *The Four Seasons* by Antonio Vivaldi, a windy fall soundscape, or fun fall music; masking tape; pictures of fall-themed activities

Using masking tape, create straight lines around the floor of the classroom, between three to five feet in length.

Tape pictures of different fall-themed activities around the classroom, next to the masking tape lines. Here are some ideas of pictures you could include:

children raking up leaves

Canadian geese flying in a V formation

families picking apples

a grizzly bear getting ready to hibernate

Allow the students to move around the classroom, taking turns walking on the different lines and pretending to act out the different autumn-themed activities as they find them on the lines. Use the music to signify when children should start moving and to let them know when to stop. You can also put children in small groups on the different lines. Let them walk the line several times before switching the groups to different lines.

Closing Circle and Cooldown (2–3 minutes)

Moving with Sheer Scarves (More recommendations for moving with scarves can be found on page 95.)

Materials: calming guitar music or other peaceful music, autumn-colored scarves

Have the children stand or sit in a circle.

Give each child a scarf. Turn on the music.

Play peekaboo using scarves.

Move the scarf as though it is blowing in a gentle breeze, then a strong wind, then a gentle breeze again.

Move the scarf like a leaf falling from a tree.

Move the scarf like a Canadian goose flying. As a class, create a flock of birds migrating for the winter.

Lift your arms up and breathe in, then move them down and breathe out, like your arms are a bird's wings. Repeat several times until the children's bodies are calm.

Reflection (1 minute or less)

Make a Face (This activity can be found on page 108.)

Have the children stand or sit in a circle.

Each child uses facial expressions to demonstrate how he felt about today's drama class.

Closing Ritual (2–3 minutes)

Encore! Take a Bow (This activity can be found on page 109.)

Have all the students stand in a circle.

Each child bows, one at a time, while the others applaud her.

Take a final bow together as a class.

Give each other a final round of applause by clapping hands while moving them in a circle.

Art Component:

Materials:

crayons without paper on them

fall leaves

newsprint

Go on a fall leaf walk and collect various fall leaves. Make rubbings of the leaves using various autumn-colored crayons.

WINTER

. . . .

Date: August 12, 2017   By: Lavinia Roberts

Theme/Learning Goals:

Children will explore the season of winter. What is the weather like? What do people
do during winter?

Materials:

white scarves, white ribbons tied to elastic wristbands, or paper snowflakes for dancing
(optional)

The Snowy Day by Ezra Jack Keats

"Waltz of the Snowflakes" from *The Nutcracker* by Pyotr Tchaikovsky

Opening Circle and Breathing Activity (2–3 minutes)

*Cool the Hot Chocolate Breath (1 minute or less) (This is a variation of "Smell the Flower/
Blow the Dandelion" on page 24.)*

Breathe in like you are smelling hot chocolate.

Breathe out like you are blowing on the hot chocolate.

Polar Bear Breath (1 minute or less)

Breathe in three times through your nose like a gruff polar bear, and breathe out like
the cold Arctic wind.

Blow out through your teeth to howl like a cold winter's wind.

See how long you can sustain your breath and create the sound of the winter's wind.

*Frosty the Snowman Breath (1 minute or less) (This is a variation of "Ha! Ha! Ho! Ho!"
found on page 26.)*

Breathe in until you fill your lungs and your tummy has expanded.

Then say "ha, ha, ha!"

Vocal Warm-up (2–3 minutes)

Winter Snow Is Falling Down

Sing to the tune of "London Bridge Is Falling Down":

Winter snow is falling down,

falling down, falling down.

Winter snow is falling down,

welcome winter.

Children can move their hands like snow falling from the sky.

Concentration, Focus, or Listening Warm-up (5–8 minutes)

Countdown (2–3 minutes) (This activity can be found on page 41.)

Tell students to stand in a circle.

The students count to ten. Beginning at one, they will be as quiet and as low to the

    ground as they can be. By ten, they will be as big and as loud as they can be.

The class then counts back down to one, getting gradually softer.

Yoga Poses (3–5 minutes) (See more yoga poses on page 45.)

Downhill Skier Pose:

Place feet together, firmly planted to the earth.

Next, bend your knees and sweep your arms back.

Snowboarder Pose (Warrior II Pose):

One leg is bent at the knee, the other stretched out behind you. The foot of the leg

    that's behind you should be turned horizontally.

Your torso is twisted; the snowboarder's arms are stretched out horizontally.

Take deep breaths of the fresh mountain air.

Ice Skater (Warrior III Pose):

One leg is firmly planted on the ground.

Next, stretch one leg back, hands extended in front of you.

Energizing Body Warm-up

Across the Classroom (This activity can be found on page 55.)

Materials: music, such as "Winter" from Antonio Vivaldi's *The Four Seasons*

    (recommended)

Line up the children along a wall, not in front of each other but spread out evenly along

    the wall.

Instruct the students in how to cross the classroom using different movements. Turn

    on the music to help create a fun and engaging environment.

Once the children reach the wall on the other side, they should wait for instructions

    about the next movement they will use to cross the classroom. Allow students to

    offer suggestions. Here are ideas for different movements the class could perform to

    cross the room:

as though they are on skis

as though they are ice skating

as though they are shivering, walking through heavy snow

as though they are walking into a strong winter wind

as though they are snowflakes twirling through the sky

as though they are pulling a sled

as through the floor is covered in slick ice

Imaginative Play Activity (5–7 minutes)

Snow Day! (This is a variation of "Jump into the Story!" found on page 154)

Materials: *The Snowy Day* by Ezra Jack Keats

Read Ezra Jack Keats's childhood classic *The Snowy Day*.

Afterward, invite the children to act out the various activities the young protagonist does in the book, from waking up to going to sleep.

Creative Movement Activity (5–7 minutes)

Let It Snow (This activity can be found on page 128.)

Materials: "Waltz of the Snowflakes" from *The Nutcracker* by Pyotr Tchaikovsky, white handkerchiefs, white ribbons tied to elastic bands (optional)

Tell the children that this music was inspired by snow falling down.

The actors can pretend that their fingertips are snowflakes falling down. They lift their arms up, then bring their hands down like snowflakes falling from the sky.

Tell them that when the music starts, they can move as snowflakes. When the music stops, they should freeze in place. Give the children white handkerchiefs or white ribbons tied to elastic bands.

Play the music and let children pretend to be snowflakes falling down to the earth while they dance to the music.

Cooldown (3–5 minutes)

Winter Wonderland Cooldown (This activity can be found on page 105.)

Have students lie down on the floor with plenty of space between them so they don't accidentally bump into one another.

Make snow angels on the floor. Breathe in when your arms and legs go up, and out when your arms and legs go down.

Then, have the children sit up and make a circle as a class, like they are warming their hands around a fire on a cold winter night.

Tell them to breathe in like they are smelling the delicious soup on the fire, then out like they are blowing on a hot bowl of soup. Have them do this a few times. You can even pretend to eat the soup.

Have the children do a deep yawn and stretch. They can imagine that they are snuggling
into warm sleeping bags, and close their eyes. Hum them a lullaby.

Tell them that when you ring your bell, they should sit up in a circle by the count of ten
so you can all return to the classroom.

Closing Circle and Reflection (3–5 minutes)

One-Word Reflection (This activity can be found on page 107.)

Have each child stand in the circle.

One at a time, ask each student to say one word to describe the day!

Closing Ritual (3–5 minutes)

Encore! Take a Bow (This activity can be found on page 109.)

Have all the students stand in a circle.

Each child bows, one at a time, while the others applaud him.

Take a final bow together as a class.

Give each other a final round of applause by clapping hands while moving them in a
circle.

Art Component:

Materials:

blue paper

white chalk or oil pastels

winter-colored geometric shapes to collage with

glue sticks

Famous artwork: *City College Is like a Beacon over Harlem* by Jacob Lawrence

Music: Antonio Vivaldi's "Winter" from *The Four Seasons*

Draw a winter wonderland as a class. Look at images of how other artists have depicted
a snowy day. Allow students to create their winter scenes on blue paper. Collage
buildings using familiar geometric shapes, and draw in snow using chalk or white oil
pastels. Play Antonio Vivaldi's "Winter" from *The Four Seasons* while the children
work.

Lesson Plan Template

SAMPLE LESSON PLAN

LESSON NAME: _____

Date: _____   By: _____

Theme/Learning Goals:

_____
_____
_____
_____

Materials:

_____
_____
_____
_____
_____
_____

Opening Circle and Breathing Activity:

_____
_____
_____
_____
_____
_____
_____
_____

Vocal Warm-up:

_____

_____

_____

_____

_____

_____

_____

_____

Concentration, Focus, or Listening Warm-up:

_____

_____

_____

_____

_____

_____

_____

_____

_____

Energizing Body Warm-up:

_____

_____

_____

_____

_____

_____

_____

_____

_____

Imaginative Play Activity:

_____

_____

_____

_____

_____

_____

_____

_____

Creative Movement Activity:

_____

_____

_____

_____

_____

_____

_____

_____

_____

_____

Cooldown:

_____

_____

_____

_____

_____

_____

_____

_____

_____

Closing Circle and Reflection:

_____

_____

_____

_____

_____

_____

_____

_____

_____

Closing Ritual:

_____

_____

_____

_____

_____

_____

_____

_____

_____

Art Component:

_____

_____

_____

_____

_____

_____

_____

_____

_____

Glossary of Terms

This glossary includes theatre terms to incorporate into your teaching practice. These definitions are adapted to fit early childhood spaces. Please feel free to incorporate them into the instructions you use with your group. Using the correct terminology during reflection or while giving instructions will teach young children about the medium of theatre that they are working in and will help them articulate their ideas and reflections during discussions in drama class. Using correct terminology also validates children's work and the medium they are working in, letting them know you value and respect theatre as an artistic medium and not just as a way to play and have fun together.

Some of the more challenging terms, such as *world of the play* or *teacher-in-role*, are provided for clarification for the reader and might not be age appropriate in an early childhood classroom. Terms such as *actor*, *bow*, or *puppet* are more age appropriate.

ACT: to make believe, pretend, and sometimes perform for others

ACTOR: a child believing, pretending, and performing

ACTOR NEUTRAL: an actor standing in a neutral position, relaxed, with good posture, ready to work

APPLAUSE: clapping for actors to express gratitude for their work

AUDIENCE: the people watching a performance

BLOCKING: the actions and staging that actors use in a performance

BOW: to bend at the waist for the audience; a way to say "thank you" and to acknowledge thanks from the audience

CAST: the actors involved in a performance

CHARACTER: a creature or person created by a child as part of a dramatic play session

CHEAT OUT: talking out to the audience instead of turning sideways to face the person you are speaking to onstage; a technique to project your voice

COSTUME: the clothing used in a performance to create a character

CREATIVE MOVEMENT: to explore a theme, environment, or feeling with the body in an expressive and imaginative way; creative movement allows children to answer kinesthetic questions through moving with their bodies

CUE: a signal, such as a line, a noise, or an action, for an action or a line of dialogue to be carried out at a specific time in a theatrical production

CURTAIN CALL: when actors come out after a performance and bow while the audience applauds

DIAPHRAGMATIC BREATHING: breathing from deep within the diaphragm; the stomach expands when you breathe in and flattens when you breathe out

DRAMATIC PLAY: a form of creative play in which children, in groups or alone, create and agree upon roles and then act them out; this type of play happens in a drama center but encompasses many kinds of make-believe

DRESS REHEARSAL: the final rehearsal of a show before the opening performance

IMPROVISATION: to create a performance by making up the dialogue and actions as you go along; improvisation involves listening, teamwork, and being bold

MAKE BELIEVE: to pretend or use one's imagination

PANTOMIME (sometimes referred to as *mime*): the theatrical technique of suggesting action, character, or emotion without words, using only gesture, expression, and movement

PROP: an object used in a performance

PUPPET: a model person or animal that is controlled by the child or teacher; there are various kinds of puppets

PUPPETEER: the person manipulating a puppet

ROLE PLAY: a type of play in which children create and act out different roles, often as part of dramatic play or during drama class

SCENERY: the backdrop of a play; in early childhood, this can be a mural the children create, chalk drawings on the ground, or other set pieces created by the children

SETTING: the imaginative world where a drama activity or play takes place

SOLITARY PLAY: when children play alone

STAGE: the area designated for the actors to perform for the audience

STAGE BUSINESS: the blocking or actions an actor performs on stage

STAGED READING: reading a play out loud without adding any blocking

STORY DRAMATIZATION: to act out a story; the story can be from a picture book, nursery rhyme, or devised by the children

TABLEAUX: children creating a still picture with their bodies

TEACHER-IN-ROLE: the teacher pretending to be a character within the make-believe world of the children's drama play or theatre activity

TROUPE: a community of actors working together to create a theatrical production

WORLD OF THE PLAY: the society, morality, psychology, and aesthetic reality of a play; every play has its own world

Bibliography

Allison, C., S. Baron-Cohen, S.J. Wheelwright, M.H. Stone, and S.J. Muncer. 2011. "Psychometric Analysis of the Empathy Quotient (EQ)." *Personality and Individual Differences* 51 (7): 829–835.

Anderson-McNamee, Jona K., and Sandra J. Bailey. 2010. "The Importance of Play in Early Childhood Development." *MontGuide* April 2010. Bozeman, MT: Montana State University Extension. www.msuextension.org/health/documents/MT201003HR .pdf.

Bredekamp, Sue, and Carol Copple, eds. 1997. *Developmentally Appropriate Practice in Early Childhood Programs.* 2nd ed. Washington, DC: NAEYC.

Dodge, Diane Trister, Laura J. Colker, and Cate Heroman. (2002). *The Creative Curriculum for Preschool.* Washington, DC: Teaching Strategies.

Epstein, Ann S. 2003. "How Planning and Reflection Develop Children's Thinking Skills." *Young Children* on the Web September 2003. http://journal.naeyc.org/btj/200309 /Planning&Reflection.pdf.

Gardner, Howard. 1983. *Frames for Mind: The Theory of Multiple Intelligences.* New York: BasicBooks.

———. 2006. *Multiple Intelligences: New Horizons.* New York: BasicBooks.

Gillespie, Linda, and Sandra Petersen. 2012. "Rituals and Routines: Supporting Infants and Toddlers and Their Families." *Young Children* 67 (4): 76–77. www.naeyc.org/yc /files/yc/file/201209/Rock-n-Roll_YC0912.pdf

Grossman, Sue. 2017. "Offering Children Choices: Encouraging Autonomy and Learning While Minimizing Conflicts." Early Childhood News. Accessed August 10. www.early childhoodnews.com/earlychildhood/article_view.aspx?ArticleID=607.

Hirsh, Rae Ann. 2004. *Early Childhood Curriculum: Incorporating Multiple Intelligences, Developmentally Appropriate Practice, and Play.* Boston: Pearson.

Kaufman, Scott Barry, Jerome L. Singer, and Dorothy G. Singer. 2012. "The Need for Pretend Play in Child Development." *Psychology Today*, March 6, 2012. www.psychology today.com/blog/beautiful-minds/201203/the-need-pretend-play-in-child-develop ment.

Kaufmann, Karen A. 2005. *Inclusive Creative Movement and Dance.* Champaign, IL: Human Kinetics.

Maxim, George W. 1997. *The Very Young: Developmental Education for the Early Years*, 5th Ed. Upper Saddle River, NJ: Merrill/Prentice Hall.

National Research Council. 2001. *Eager to Learn: Educating Our Preschoolers.* Edited by Barbara T. Bowman, M. Suzanne Donovan, and M. Susan Burns. Committee on Early

Childhood Pedagogy. Commission on Behavioral and Social Sciences and Education. Washington, DC: National Academy Press. www.nap.edu/read/9745/chapter/1.

Ostrosky, M.M., and E.Y. Jung. "Building Positive Teacher-Child Relationships." *What Works Briefs* 12. Center on the Social and Emotional Foundations for Early Learning, http://csefel.vanderbilt.edu/briefs/wwb12.pdf.

Parsai, Parvin. 2014. "A Case Study of Preschool Children Exhibiting Prosocial and Empathic Behaviors During Sociodramatic Play." Doctorate thesis, University of Toledo. Theses and Dissertations (1666). http://utdr.utoledo.edu/theses-dissertations /1666.

Poole, Carla, Susan A. Miller, and Ellen Booth Church. "Ages & Stages: All About Body Awareness." *Early Childhood Today* by Scholastic. Accessed August 10. www .scholastic.com/teachers/articles/teaching-content/ages-stages-all-about-body -awareness/.

Preusse, Kathy. 2017 "Fostering Prosocial Behavior in Young Children." EarlyChildhood News.com. Accessed August 10. www.earlychildhoodnews.com/earlychildhood/article _view.aspx?ArticleId=566.

Reedy, Patricia. 2003. *Body, Mind, & Spirit in Action: A Teacher's Guide to Creative Dance.* Berkeley: Luna Kids Dance.

Useful Resources

California Department of Education. 2011. *The California Preschool Curriculum Framework, Volume 2.* Edited by Faye Ong and John McLean. Sacramento: California Department of Education.

Colorado Preschool Program Staff. 2012. "Preschool Drama and Theatre Arts Academic Standards in High Quality Early Childhood Care and Education Settings." Colorado Department of Education. www.cde.state.co.us/sites/default/files/documents/cpp /download/standards/prek_drama_in_high_quality_settings.pdf.

Crepeau, Ingrid M., and M. Ann Richards. 2003. *A Show of Hands: Using Puppetry with Young Children.* St. Paul, MN: Redleaf Press.

Kacev, Glenda, and Sylvia Roth. 2011. *Bal Yoga for Kids.*

New Jersey Department of Education. 2014. *2014 Preschool Learning and Teaching Standards.* Trenton: New Jersey Department of Education.

Singleton, Mark. 2016. *Yoga for You and Your Child: The Step-by-Step Guide to Enjoying Yoga with Children of All Ages.* London: Watkins.

Task Force on Children's Learning and the Arts: Birth to Age Eight. 1998. *Young Children and The Arts: Making Creative Connections.* Washington, DC: Arts Education Partnership.